THE WAY
PEOPLE
LIVE

Life of a Medieval Knight

Titles in The Way People Live series include:

Cowboys in the Old West
Games of Ancient Rome
Life Among the Great Plains Indians
Life Among the Ibo Women of
  Nigeria
Life Among the Indian Fighters
Life Among the Pirates
Life Among the Samurai
Life Among the Vikings
Life During the Black Death
Life During the Crusades
Life During the French Revolution
Life During the Gold Rush
Life During the Great Depression
Life During the Middle Ages
Life During the Renaissance
Life During the Russian Revolution
Life During the Spanish Inquisition
Life in a Japanese American Internment
  Camp
Life in a Medieval Castle
Life in a Medieval Monastery
Life in a Nazi Concentration Camp
Life in a Wild West Show
Life in Ancient Athens
Life in Ancient China
Life in Ancient Egypt
Life in Ancient Greece

Life in Ancient Rome
Life in Charles Dickens's England
Life in Communist Russia
Life in Genghis Khan's Mongolia
Life in the Amazon Rain Forest
Life in the American Colonies
Life in the Elizabethan Theater
Life in the Hitler Youth
Life in the North During the Civil War
Life in the South During the Civil War
Life in the Warsaw Ghetto
Life in Moscow
Life in Tokyo
Life in War-Torn Bosnia
Life of a Medieval Knight
Life of a Nazi Soldier
Life of a Roman Slave
Life of a Roman Soldier
Life of a Slave on a Southern Plantation
Life on Alcatraz
Life on a Medieval Pilgrimage
Life on an African Slave Ship
Life on an Everest Expedition
Life on Ellis Island
Life on the American Frontier
Life on the Oregon Trail
Life on the Underground Railroad
Life Under the Jim Crow Laws

THE WAY PEOPLE LIVE

Life of a Medieval Knight

by
James A. Corrick

Lucent Books, P.O. Box 289011, San Diego, CA 92198-9011

For Pat, the other James in the Family

Library of Congress Cataloging-in-Publication Data

Corrick, James A.
  Life of a Medieval knight / by James A. Corrick.
      p. cm. — (The way people live)
Includes bibliographical references and index.
Summary: Discusses feudalism, chivalry, clothing and weaponry, practices of
war, the Crusades, tournaments and other aspects of the lives of noble soldiers
of the Middle Ages.
  ISBN 1-56006-817-5 (alk. paper)
  1. Knights and knighthood—Europe—History—Juvenile literature. 2.
Civilization, Medieval—Juvenile literature. 3. Chivalry—Europe—History—
Juvenile literature. [1. Knights and knighthood. 2. Civilization, Medieval. 3.
Chivalry.] I. Title. II. Series.
  CR4513 .C67 2001
  940.1—dc21

00-011303

Contents

Discovering the Humanity in Us All

Books in The Way People Live series focus on groups of people in a wide variety of circumstances, settings, and time periods. Some books focus on different cultural groups, others, on people in a particular historical time period, while others cover people involved in a specific event. Each book emphasizes the daily routines, personal and historical struggles, and achievements of people from all walks of life.

To really understand any culture, it is necessary to strip the mind of the common notions we hold about groups of people. These stereotypes are the archenemies of learning. It does not even matter whether the stereotypes are positive or negative; they are confining and tight. Removing them is a challenge that's not easily met, as anyone who has ever tried it will admit. Ideas that do not fit into the templates we create are unwelcome visitors—ones we would prefer remain quietly in a corner or forgotten room.

The cowboy of the Old West is a good example of such confining roles. The cowboy was courageous, yet soft-spoken. His time (it is always a he, in our template) was spent alternatively saving a rancher's daughter from certain death on a runaway stagecoach, or shooting it out with rustlers. At times, of course, he was likely to get a little crazy in town after a trail drive, but for the most part, he was the epitome of inner strength. It is disconcerting to find out that the cowboy is human, even a bit childish. Can it really be true that cowboys would line up to help the cook on the trail drive grind coffee, just hoping he would give them a little stick of peppermint candy that came with the coffee shipment? The idea of tough cowboys vying with one another to help "Coosie" (as they called their cooks) for a bit of candy seems silly and out of place.

So is the vision of Eskimos playing video games and watching MTV, living in prefab housing in the Arctic. It just does not fit with what "Eskimo" means. We are far more comfortable with snow igloos and whale blubber, harpoons and kayaks.

Although the cultures dealt with in Lucent's The Way People Live series are often historically and socially well known, the emphasis is on the personal aspects of life. Groups of people, while unquestionably affected by their politics and their governmental structures, are more than those institutions. How do people in a particular time and place educate their children? What do they eat? And how do they build their houses? What kinds of work do they do? What kinds of games do they enjoy? The answers to these questions bring these cultures to life. People's lives are revealed in the particulars and only by knowing the particulars can we understand these cultures' will to survive and their moments of weakness and greatness.

This is not to say that understanding politics does not help to understand a culture. There is no question that the Warsaw ghetto, for example, was a culture that was brought about by the politics and social ideas of Adolf

Hitler and the Third Reich. But the Jews who were crowded together in the ghetto cannot be understood by the Reich's politics. Their life was a day-to-day battle for existence, and the creativity and methods they used to prolong their lives is a vital story of human perseverance that would be denied by focusing only on the institutions of Hitler's Germany. Knowing that children as young as five or six outwitted Nazi guards on a daily basis, that Jewish policemen helped the Germans control the ghetto, that children attended secret schools in the ghetto and even earned diplomas—these are the things that reveal the fabric of life, that can inspire, intrigue, and amaze.

Books in The Way People Live series allow both the casual reader and the student to see humans as victims, heroes, and onlookers. And although humans act in ways that can fill us with feelings of sorrow and revulsion, it is important to remember that "hero," "predator," and "victim" are dangerous terms. Heaping undue pity or praise on people reduces them to objects, and strips them of their humanity.

Seeing the Jews of Warsaw only as victims is to deny their humanity. Seeing them only as they appear in surviving photos, staring at the camera with infinite sadness, is limiting, both to them and to those who want to understand them. To an object of pity, the only appropriate response becomes "Those poor creatures!" and that reduces both the quality of their struggle and the depth of their despair. No one is served by such two-dimensional views of people and their cultures.

With this in mind, The Way People Live series strives to flesh out the traditional, two-dimensional views of people in various cultures and historical circumstances. Using a wide variety of primary quotations—the words not only of the politicians and government leaders, but of the real people whose lives are being examined—each book in the series attempts to show an honest and complete picture of a culture removed from our own by time or space.

By examining cultures in this way, the reader will notice not only the glaring differences from his or her own culture, but also will be struck by the similarities. For indeed, people share common needs—warmth, good company, stability, and affirmation from others. Ultimately, seeing how people really live, or have lived, can only enrich our understanding of ourselves.

The Coming of the Knight

Medieval knights were first and foremost warriors, whose heyday was the late Middle Ages: the twelfth through the fourteenth centuries. Dominating the medieval battlefield during these years, they fought from horseback, wore body-covering armor, and used many weapons, most notably the sword and the lance. Their skills at riding and in the use of weapons came from years of training.

In addition to fighting, many knights managed large farming estates, known as manors, which were important food producers in England and western Europe. These landholding knights also took a hand in local governments; indeed, they frequently were the local governments. Their advice on matters both military and civilian was sought by higher ranking nobles and by kings.

Other, landless knights made a living as mercenaries in local wars. Like landed knights, they also took part in tournaments, or mock combats, in which the winners collected money from the losers. Some of these wanderers joined religious orders of knights and journeyed to the Near East, defending Christian holdings in the region. Still others became popular poets, known as troubadours.

Troubled Times

Knights were a product of the Middle Ages, which began about A.D. 500, after the fall of the Roman Empire, and lasted until about 1500, the start of the Renaissance. The first five centuries of the period, from 500 to 1000, were filled with violence as peoples

Medieval knights were well-trained soldiers who dominated the battlefield during the late Middle Ages.

Mounted knights, such as the one depicted on this fourteenth-century fresco, had become the most important warriors by the beginning of the eleventh century.

from eastern Europe, Scandanavia, and North Africa invaded lands formerly held by the Romans.

Mounted Warriors

The knight emerged out of the violent early Middle Ages, for kings needed to protect themselves and their territories, and well-trained fighters became the lifeblood of kingdoms.

By the beginning of the eleventh century, kings in battle had come to depend less on foot soldiers and more on heavily armed and armored warriors mounted on horses. Forming a line and with spears leveled, armored cavalry could chase down and ride over infantry troops. The cavalry charge became the backbone of medieval tactics, and the knight became the most important soldier on the battlefield.

Horsemen and Servants

In most European languages, the word for knight came from the local word for horse, reflecting the knight's importance as a horse soldier. Thus in France, Italy, and Spain, a knight was called a chevalier, a cavaliere, and a caballero, respectively. In Germany, the knight was a ritter, from the German word for ride.

The English word "knight," however, comes from an Anglo-Saxon word for servant. This title revealed the humble beginnings of many knights prior to the eleventh century. Although some knights came from aristocratic families, most early knights, like foot soldiers, were freeborn peasants. In fact, in Germany, many of the first knights were not even freeborn. According to the scholar Frances Gies, these German knights "were subject to the same taxes as serfs, . . . could not acquire or sell property without their lord's consent, and could even be bought and sold."[1]

During the eleventh century, however, the military importance of the knight began thrusting all knights, even in Germany, into the aristocracy. By the twelfth century, knights had not just become a part of the aristocracy, they were the aristocracy. Kings were knights, and so were high-ranking nobles, such as dukes, counts, and barons. Most knights, however, occupied the lowest rung of the aristocratic ladder and had no other title except knight. But no matter what the rank, to be a knight was to be a noble.

Brothers in Arms

With their rise to the aristocracy came a change in the way knights viewed themselves. They were no longer mere soldiers but brothers in arms, members of an elite class of warriors. Their attitude is summed up well by Gutierre Díaz de Gómez in his fifteenth-century biography of the knight Pero Niño: "a brave man, mounted on a good horse, may do more in an hour of fighting than ten or mayhap [perhaps] a hundred could afoot. For this reason do men rightly call him knight."[2]

Knights almost universally enjoyed the same sports, particularly hunting and the mock combat of tournaments which they saw as crucial for maintaining their battle readiness. The thirteenth-century Spanish knight Ramón Llull wrote that

> Knights should . . . take part in tournaments. They should hunt deer, boar, and other wild animals, for in doing such things, they exercise their skill in arms, so that they are able to carry out their duties as knights.[3]

Feudalism

During the eleventh and twelfth centuries, when knights rose to greatness, money was scarce in western and central Europe. Thus kings could not afford to support the great number of knights and horses needed to defend a kingdom.

But if these rulers were short of cash, they had plenty of land. The solution then was to give as many knights as possible land grants called fiefs, which they could exploit to earn their keep. Thus, in exchange for land, the knight provided military service when needed. This cooperative bargain between kings or other nobles, called lords, and subject knights, known as vassals, was the heart of feudalism. And the manor fief was the knight's home base.

The Manor Fief

The most common fief was a manor, and the income of the vassal who held it came from rents paid by the farmworkers living on the estate. The rents generally came in the form of crops and livestock, which the landlord knight could sell or keep for his own use. Any surplus production on the estate also belonged to the knight.

A knight who was a high-ranking noble, such as a count or a baron, received from the king a manor that measured thousands of acres and centered on a castle. Along with the fief, the king often gave the knight permission to make his own laws and run his own courts.

The land grant of a high-ranking knight was so large that he in turn took vassals of his own, giving them parcels of his land to hold. In the twelfth century, for example, Count Robert of Flanders, a vassal of the king of France, had over a thousand knights in vassalage to himself. Each parcel was a smaller

The farm workers on a manor fief usually paid their rents in the form of crops and livestock, which the landlord knight could sell or keep for his own use.

manor of no more than a few hundred acres, which spread out from a fortified house, which was the residence of an ordinary knight and his household.

Other Fiefs

A fief did not have to be a large tract of land. It could be anything that generated revenue: a mill for grinding grain, a house that could be rented, or a toll bridge. Although most fiefs were based on land, in a few cases, a knight's fief had nothing to do with real property, consisting instead of the right to gather taxes,

coin money, or assign and collect fines. And some vassal knights, who lived with their lord and were known as household knights, received actual money as their fief.

Still, the overwhelming majority of vassal knights received land fiefs, and by the end of the twelfth century, most of the land of western and central Europe was in the hands of knights.

Fiefs, whether land grants or money, were passed from a father to his eldest son and often remained in the same family's hands for centuries. The knight's heir had to pay his lord a form of inheritance tax called relief, perhaps the amount of money the fief produced in a year. For vassals who died without heirs, the fief was the lord's to dispose of as he saw fit.

Feudal Rights and Duties

Under feudalism both the lord and the vassal had duties and rights. A lord promised to protect his vassal knight's fief, by going to war if necessary. The lord also guaranteed that a vassal accused of any crime would have the chance to plead his case before his social equals, or peers.

In return, the vassal knight pledged to give advice about military and political matters both to the lord and to other vassals of the lord. The knight also promised to provide his lord with aid, particularly military. Thus, if his lord commanded, a vassal had to go to war, mounted and fully equipped with armor and weapons.

Additionally, the vassal knight might be called upon to supply his lord with food or lodging if the higher ranking nobleman happened to pass through the vassal's fief. The lord could also ask his vassal for money.

Emergencies, long wars, or important ceremonial events, such as the knighting of the lord's oldest son or the marriage of his eldest daughter, called for such financial aid.

Knights for Hire

Fiefs were the major source of income for knights well into the thirteenth century, but many knights were unable to gain a fief because there were more knights than fiefs. All sons of a knight could, and often did, become knights. However, only one son could inherit the father's fief. Further, new fiefs were increasingly difficult to find after about a century of feudalism, since by then most land had been granted to vassals.

By the thirteenth century, however, money was becoming more plentiful in Europe owing to increased trade, particularly with the Near East. Thus, many fiefless knights were being paid salaries to fight as mercenaries for kings and high-ranking nobles. But whether a knight's income came from a fief or from wages, he was responsible for supplying his own armor, weapons, and horse.

The Outfitting of the Knight

The armor, weapons, and horses of a knight set him apart from all other fighting men of the Middle Ages. As a nameless poet of the Middle Ages wrote, "horse, shield, spear, helmet and sword/These make a good knight's value."[4] The knight was more heavily armored and armed than any of his opponents on foot. His equipment was designed so that, with the help of a warhorse, he could deliver a shattering blow to enemy troops, infantry, and enemy cavalry alike.

The Cost of Outfitting

Good armor and good weapons required time and money to make. The raw materials, iron and steel, a hardened form of iron, did not come cheap.

Steel was particularly expensive because it had to be made in limited amounts, for the lengthy, high-temperature process was barely within the reach of medieval European technology. Indeed, Europe did not produce enough steel to meet the demands of weapons and armor makers, and consequently, much of it was imported from India and Persia, adding to the cost.

Labor to make armor and weapons was not cheap either, since such metalwork required skilled craftsmen. Local blacksmiths occasionally made both weapons and armor for knights of a particular region, and some wealthy knights had their own armorers, or

Skilled craftsmen used expensive materials such as iron and steel to produce the armor and weapons of the medieval knight.

specialists in arms and armor manufacture. However, the best equipment came from certain areas of Europe. German armor was highly prized, as was that from Italy. In particular, armor from Milan, was valued for its fine craftsmanship and ruggedness. The price of imported armor was very high.

Footing the Bill

Thus, outfitting a knight was a costly business. To equip himself fully and maintain that equipment, as well as keep one or more horses, a knight had to have as much money as was generated yearly by a manor of some four hundred acres. By the 1400s, the price of armor alone easily cost a quarter of a knight's annual income, while a good warhorse represented as much as a year's income.

And it was up to each of these mounted warriors to pay for his own equipment, either from his earnings as a fief holder or his wages as a mercenary. Since no lord would take on a vassal or hire a knight who was not fully equipped and horsed, young knights received these necessities from their families.

Mail

By the late Middle Ages, a knight's armor consisted of two layers: a metal mesh, known as mail or chain mail, was covered by solid metal pieces, known as plate armor.

Hundreds, sometimes thousands, of small interlocking metal rings made up mail. Each of these rings was connected to four others. Like all knightly accessories, mail was expensive, and therefore it was often passed down from father to son and refitted to each new wearer by adding or subtracting links.

The knight portrayed in this illustration is wearing chain mail, an armor that was made up of many small interlocking rings.

Several pieces of mail were needed to protect the knight. On his head, he wore a coif, which was like a ski mask made of mail. An opening in the front left the eyes, nose, and mouth exposed. A long mail shirt, known as a hauberk, covered the torso and arms, sometimes stretching to the knees. The hauberk, made from some thirty thousand metal rings and weighing twenty pounds, was slit below the waist, front and back, to allow for riding. Some of these mail shirts were made by sewing the metal rings onto a linen backing rather than interlinking them. A knight's hands were protected by mail mittens, sometimes attached to the hauberk's sleeves, while his legs and feet were covered by mail hose, or chausses.

The Weakness of Mail

Until the thirteenth century, mail was the sole armor of knights and it kept a knight from being sliced open by sword cuts. Its protection was limited, however. Mail did not prevent sword blows from bruising badly, breaking bones, or producing nasty wounds by driving the mail links into the body. Internal bleeding from such blows was also a danger.

In addition, mail was not good protection against arrows, particularly those shot from the powerful English longbow, or against missiles fired by crossbows. The yard-long, steel-tipped arrow propelled by a longbow could travel almost a quarter-mile. At half that distance, it could easily drive its way through mail. Even some less powerful bows could pierce mail at a shorter distances.

The longbow was mainly an English weapon, rarely used by other European soldiers, and it took years of practice to master. The crossbow was much easier to use, and although it had a much shorter range than the longbow, its short wooden or iron arrow, called a quarrel or bolt, could also drive through mail. The crossbow had a bow mounted flat and at a right angle to a long piece of wood, the stock. When loading, a

Arms and Armor

The anonymous Spanish author of the twelfth-century *Poem of the Cid*, gives a dramatic and accurate portrait of the effectiveness of medieval weapons and armor in his description of the following combat.

"[The opponents] hugged their shields over their hearts, lowered the lances wrapped in their pennons [streamers], bent their faces over their saddles, dug their spurs into their horses, and the earth shook as they leapt forward. . . .

Pedro Bermúdez . . . came face to face with Fernando González . . . [who] pierced Don Pedro's shield but drove through upon nothing and touched no flesh, and in two places the shaft of his spear [lance] snapped. Pedro Bermúdez remained firm [in his saddle], . . . and he struck . . . [a blow that] burst the shield [of Fernando] . . . and broke it apart, . . . [then] drove his lance through to the breast close to the heart. Fernando was wearing three suits of chain mail and this saved him; two folds were pierced and the third held firm, but the mail and the tunic . . . were driven . . . into the flesh, so that the blood ran from Fernando's mouth, and the [saddle] girth broke. . . . Fernando was flung to the ground. . . .

Don Martin and Diego González struck with their spears; such were the blows that both [lances] were broken. Martin . . . set hand on his sword. . . . It struck a blow which caught him [Diego] from the side; it split apart the top of his helmet and it broke all the buckles; it sheared the head mail . . . razed [sliced] the hair of the head and came to the flesh; part [of which] fell to the field, the rest remained."

crossbowman had to put the head of the stock on the ground and then, either by hand or with a crank, pull back on the bowstring until he could slip it over a latch. The user then inserted a bolt and released the bolt by pulling on a trigger.

The effectiveness of these weapons was well illustrated by the fate of a fourteenth-century Swedish army. Stephen Turnbull writes that:

> In 1361 a Danish royal army slaughtered . . . [an] army of Swedish peasants and townsmen. . . . The sole protection for the Swedes was mail, and after the battle their bodies were heaped into a mass grave. Excavations of the grave during the 1930s revealed that at least 125 men had suffered fatal head wounds from arrows and crossbow bolts which had struck their mail hoods. In many cases the arrowheads were found inside the skulls.[5]

Plate Armor

Thus, a need for a better defense against powerfully propelled missiles led to the use of plate armor in the thirteenth century. Each plate was made from solid iron or steel, curved to fit the torso, groin, arms, and legs and worn over the mail. The pieces for the arms and legs looked something like gutter piping. Metal gloves protected the hands and metal shoes the feet.

Full suits of plate were not common until the very end of the medieval period. The more usual practice was to use plate to reinforce special danger points, such as the torso, elbows, kneecaps, and sometimes, the legs, which were always at risk of injury from attacks by infantrymen hacking away at

Plate armor was made from solid iron or steel, providing medieval knights with protection from projectiles.

knights from the ground. The force of the blows landing on solid plate spread out through the metal, thereby loosing much of its force in comparison to the often deadly wounds received by knights who wore mail alone.

The Helmet

Topping the armor of the knight was a helmet. Like the rest of his protective gear, it was made of iron or steel. Helmets sometimes were padded to soften the force of blows to the head.

One of the favorite helmets of the thirteenth and fourteenth centuries was a flat-topped cylinder that extended down over the head to the neck. In some versions of this helmet, known as the great helm, the knight's face was left exposed. More commonly, the entire head, including the face, was enclosed by the helm. Eye slits provided vision, while holes at nose and mouth levels let in air. Some of these helmets had a visor, a hinged front section, that a knight could raise when not in battle.

The flat-topped helm had a serious flaw. A strong enough cut from a sword or a battle-ax could split both helmet and knight's skull. Consequently, many knights came to prefer a tapered top to their helms since such a curving surface deflected weapon blows better.

An additional protective device on the top of many helms was a raised section, known as a crest. This protrusion helped lessen or deflect the blows of swords and other weapons. The earliest crests were fairly simple metal ridges, sometimes with sawlike teeth. Later, they became objects of decoration, such as

This medieval helmet features a visor, a hinged front section that the knight could raise after battle, and a curved top to deflect weapon blows.

small, brightly painted leather models of birds or animals.

Little could be done, however, to correct the weakest point of a knight's helmet, the eye slit. Knights always risked being killed by an arrow or a sword driving through this opening. The fourteenth-century chronicler Jean Froissart wrote that the English knight John Chandos died of a sword "stroke [that] entered into the flesh under his eye between the nose and the forehead . . . and entered into his brain."[6]

Getting Dressed

Before putting on his armor, a knight dressed in a long-sleeved woolen shirt. He then slipped into short linen pants and stockings. Finally, he pulled on an aketon, a knee-length coat. The aketon, which was either padded cloth or made of leather, protected the knight from the chafing caused by the movement of his armor. His arms, legs, and feet were similarly protected by shirt sleeves and stockings. A padded cap, known as an arming cap, was frequently worn to cushion the head from the heavy mail coif and helmet.

In putting on his mail, a knight found it best to have help from his squire (a trainee serving an apprenticeship under the knight). The hauberk, particularly a long one, was difficult to wiggle into without assistance. Some, like modern hospital gowns, were open in the back and easy enough to get into. Lacing the back panels together was best done by the squire.

After the mail was in place, the knight put on his plate armor. Each piece of plate was fastened on with straps, and the squire normally tightened the plate fittings.

Over the armor, the knight wore a surcoat, a sleeveless linen tunic that, like the

The knight often required the assistance of a squire when putting on cumbersome pieces of armor such as the hauberk.

hauberk, was slit front and back for riding. This garment protected the hauberk from rusting in wet weather and in hot weather kept the knight cooler than he would have been with the sun beating directly down on plate metal garments.

If a knight did not wear plate below the waist, he had no footwear other than the mail that protected his feet. A full set of plate came with a set of metal shoes. On his heels, whether mailed or plated, a knight fastened gold-plated iron spurs.

Sheathed in Armor

In general, mail plus plate armor protected the knight well, as long as he remained on his horse. However, once off his horse—either to fight on foot or because his horse had been killed or injured—he could fall victim to more lightly armored foot soldiers.

The problem for the dismounted knight was that his armor was not designed for easy movement on foot. Consequently, enemy troopers could outmaneuver him, slipping a dagger or a sword between his plates, and with a strong enough thrust, breaking the mail links beneath. Froissart described how English infantry killed many unhorsed French knights in this manner during the 1346 Battle of Crécy:

> The sharp arrows ran into the men of arms [French knights] and into their horses, and many fell . . . , and when they were down, they could not relieve [rise] again, the press [crowd] was so thick that one overthrew another. . . . Among the Englishmen there were certain [soldiers] . . . that went afoot with great knives, and they went in among the men at arms, and slew . . . many.[7]

Another problem for a knight encased in plate and mail was overheating. In a fierce fight a knight in even a partial suit of plate could easily grow too hot to function effectively. He might well escape wounds, but he was often so weakened by heat exhaustion and dehydration that he could not escape being captured.

The Shield

The knight did not depend solely upon armor for protection in battle but also carried a shield. The shield had a thin wooden body, over whose outside surface was stretched canvas. Over the canvas was fastened a leather covering. On the inside, the shield had two straps for the knight's forearm and a grip for his hand, as well as a pad for the arm. A third, longer strap allowed the shield to be slung around the knight's neck when not in use.

The shield was triangular, measuring some thirty inches in height and twenty-three in width. It was also curved so that a knight could pull it close around his upper body.

A Knight's Sword

A knight used his shield to cover his left side. To protect his right, he depended upon a weapon. (Until the last two centuries of the medieval period, all knights were right-handed because, during the Middle Ages, left-handed people were considered to be children of the devil.) The type and number of weapons depended on a knight's preference and training. The anonymous author of the fifteenth-century "Manual of Arms for the Axe" called for "the axe, . . . lance, dagger, great sword and small sword, to defend oneself and resist one's . . . enemies."[8]

The guard of a medieval knight's broadsword ran at right angles to the meeting of the blade and hilt, giving the weapon the appearance of a cross.

All knights carried swords, of which the most common was the broadsword, named for its long two-edged, broad blade. The blade had a central core made of iron rods twisted together, over which was laid a steel outer covering. Smiths often cut a groove lengthwise down the middle of both sides of the blade, making the blade lighter in weight without diminishing its strength. The final blade was strong, supple, and easily sharpened.

The blade, sometimes decorated with inlays of copper or bronze, and even occasionally with gold and silver, fitted into the hilt, which provided the knight with a grip. The hilt was made from wood or bone, with a cloth or leather wrapping. At a right angle to the meeting of blade and hilt was a guard,

which protected the hand and gave the broadsword a crosslike appearance. At the end of the hilt was an iron knob, the pommel, that counterbalanced the weight of the blade.

The sword was carried in a scabbard made of leather fastened to a wooden frame. The scabbard was attached to a leather belt that went around the knight's waist, allowing the sheath to hang along his leg. Some belts let the scabbard hang straight down, while others angled the sheath so that the sword's hilt projected forward for readier access.

The average broadsword was two and a half feet long, weighed three pounds, and was easily swung one-handed by a knight. A larger and heavier version of the broadsword was

Medieval Swordsmanship

In an untitled fourteenth-century manual, accessible at www.thehaca.com/pdf/Ringeck.htm, Grand Fechtmeister (Master of the Fight) Johann Liechtenauer and his later commentator, Sigmund Ringeck, provide instruction in the use of the medieval sword.

"The first tenet of the . . . sword . . . [is] learn to strike blows equally well from both sides. . . .

If you want to strike from . . . your right side, make sure, your left foot is forward . . . ; if you want to strike from the left side, the right foot must be forward. . . .

If you strike an . . . [overhand blow] from the right side, then follow the blow with your right foot. If you do not, the blow is wrong and ineffective, because your right side stays behind. Because of this the blow will fall short and cannot travel in its proper arc towards the left side. . . .

When you are closing to an opponent, do not . . . wait for what he might use against you. Because . . . those, who just wait for their opponent's blows and do not do anything else than warding them off, do not succeed very often. . . .

Always . . . [use] all of your strength! When you are close, strike at his [your opponent's] head and at his body. . . .

If you are . . . right-handed . . . ,and you are closing to an opponent and you think you can hit him, do not strike the first blow from . . . (your) left side. Because you are weak there and you cannot resist, if he binds [exerts pressure with his sword] strongly against your blade. Because of this, strike from the right side, you can work strongly and you can use all the techniques you like. . . . If you are left-handed, do not strike from the right side."

A thirteenth-century manuscript illumination of medieval knights battling with swords.

The lance was one of the medieval knight's deadliest weapons, capable of piercing through the shield and armor of an enemy.

over a yard in length and weighed some eight pounds, requiring two hands to swing.

A broadsword was not primarily a thrusting weapon, being designed to hack and cut with the edge of the blade. A trained swordsman swung it in smooth, easy, sweeping arcs. Toward the end of the thirteenth century, smaller, thrusting swords with sharp, narrow points, came into use. Armed with this sword, a knight could either stab through his enemy's rings of mail, breaking them apart, or he could drive the blade between the joints of his opponent's plate armor.

The Lance

Knights also routinely carried a lance, which was a long, tapered spear. Made of wood, such as ash or pine, the lance was twelve feet long and tipped with a sharp metal head. A disk-shaped guard protected the knight's

hand. A foot or so of the lance extended back behind the guard.

In battle, a knight would grasp the lance just behind the guard, tucking the rear length up under his right arm so that it was pinned between arm and body. Any blow with the lance would naturally drive it backward, and to keep it from being pushed back under the knight's arm, a ring, called a grabber, encircled the lance just behind the knight's hand. The grabber stopped the lance's backward motion by jamming up against the knight's armpit.

The lance was one of the deadliest weapons in a knight's arsenal. Propelled with the force due to the combined weight of rider and horse, the lance could easily pierce right through shield, plate, hauberk, and deep into an enemy's body. The resulting wound was frequently fatal, and death occurred instantly. An accurate description of the power of a well-aimed lance is found in the anonymous medieval epic *The Song of Roland*: "Malquiant . . . charges against [Count] Anseis and strikes him on the shield. He cuts through . . . [the shield], breaks . . . his [Anseis's] hauberk and jams into the body both the head and the shaft of his spear [lance]. The Count is dead."[9]

Delivering such a deadly blow to an opponent often left the victor without a lance. To retrieve his weapon, which was now deeply embedded in the loser's body, a knight would have to tug it out of the corpse. During battle, there was not always time for such an action.

A knight could also lose his lance by breaking it. If he did not hit his enemy just right, his lance would bow up against his foe's shield or armor until it snapped in two.

The Remaining Arsenal

Upon losing his lance, a knight drew either his sword or one of the other hand weapons he carried. Some knights, for instance, also carried a battle-ax, a powerful cutting weapon that in the hands of an expert could shatter mail and even slice through a helmet and plate armor. Also favored by some was the mace, or club, which had a steel head mounted on a thick wooden handle. The head could be flanged, that is, capped with a series of projecting edges, or it could be ball-shaped with studs or spikes projecting from it. A variation on the mace was the war-flail, consisting of a spiked ball connected to a handle by an

Knightly Combat

The fourteenth-century writer Jean Froissart in his *Chronicles* gives this account of a fight between an English knight, Sir Matthew Redman, and his Scottish opponent, Sir James Lindsay, during the Battle of Otterburn.

"Sir James, to win honor, followed in chase Sir Matthew Redman, and came . . . near him. . . . Then he said: 'Ah, sir knight, turn; it is a shame thus to fly: I am James of Lindsay: if ye will not turn, I shall strike you on the back with my spear [lance].' Sir Matthew spake no word, but . . . at last Sir Matthew Redman's horse foundered and fell under him. Then he stept forth on the earth and drew out his sword, and took courage to defend himself; and the Scot thought to have stricken [struck] him on the breast, but Sir Matthew Redman

swerved from the stroke, and the spear-point entered into the earth. Then Sir Matthew strake [cut] asunder the spear with his sword; and when Sir James Lindsay saw how he had lost his spear, he cast away the truncheon [broken lance] and lighted afoot, and took a little battle-axe that he carried at his back and handled it with his one hand quickly and deliverly [skillfully] . . . and then he set at Sir Matthew and he [Sir Matthew] defended himself properly. Thus they tourneyed [fought] together, one with an axe and the other with a sword, a long season [for a long time], and no man to let [stop] them. Finally Sir James Lindsay gave the knight such strokes . . . that he [Sir Matthew] was put out of breath in such wise that he yielded himself, and said: 'Sir James Lindsay, I yield me to you.'"

Archers such as the ones depicted in the foreground of this manuscript illumination were not knights, but common foot soldiers.

iron chain. Both mace and flail could deliver mail-breaking, plate-smashing, and bone-splintering blows, and the mace was capable of crushing a helmet and the skull beneath it.

Many knights also carried daggers. Belted to the side opposite the sword, the dagger was considered a weapon of last resort, to be used when swords and other weapons were lost or broken. It was also used when knights found themselves grappling in hand-to-hand combat.

Two weapons not used by knights in battle were bows and crossbows. Both were considered unknightly, although most knights used a bow in hunting. Consequently, these weapons were assigned to the common foot soldier.

A Knight and His Horses

Armor and weapons were crucially important to a knight, but nothing was more important than his horse. Without a horse, he was equal to a foot soldier.

When a knight could afford it, he owned several horses, each for a different task. Into battle, he rode a destrier, or charger, a large, well-trained warhorse. For hunting or for traveling, he used a smaller horse, the palfrey. Additionally, he had horses for his servants and for his baggage. All the horses a knight actually rode were male because these mounted warriors considered it humiliating to ride a mare.

The Warhorse

The origin of the destrier is unknown, although the breed was probably in part Arabian stock. Weighing between fifteen hundred and two thousand pounds, the destrier stood some five feet at the shoulder. For much of the Middle Ages, the best chargers came from northwest France and from Spain. Destriers were also imported to western Europe from as far away as Turkey.

Since a knight's occupation and even his life depended on his warhorse, he chose it carefully, picking his destrier for courage, strength, and endurance. A knight had to have a horse that would not hesitate to charge into the noise and chaos of the battlefield. He also needed a horse that could be guided by pressure from the knees and spurs, since the rider's hands were usually occupied with shield and weapons.

A Horse's Strength

The destrier had to be strong enough to carry his fully armed and armored rider at a gallop. A full suit of plate plus the underlying mail was heavy, in total weighing some sixty pounds, which is roughly equal to the weight of a modern infantry soldier's pack and equipment.

Adding to the weight of rider and armor were the shield and various weapons, as well as the horse's own armor. A mail robe, or caparison, draped over the destrier's body, and a faceplate, as well as neck and back plates, provided additional protection. Many knights, however, preferred using leather or quilted caparisons and faceplates because the weight of the metal armor tired their horses too rapidly.

In addition to armor, a destrier had its iron horseshoes as weapons. Trained to rise up on their hind legs, some horses would beat about themselves with their front feet. A blow from one of these iron-clad hooves could crush an infantryman's helmet and skull or cave in his chest. Sometimes, knights would add cleats to their horses' shoes or sharpen the edges.

The Death of Horses

Despite the use of caparisons and protective plates, chargers were often killed or badly injured in battle. A knight who missed an enemy rider with his lance sometimes impaled the man's horse instead. Infantry soldiers frequently slashed at the unarmored legs and bellies of horses. And, for archers and crossbowmen, horses made much larger and easier targets than riders.

Another danger to horses was the caltrop. Infantry scattered this small, four-spiked device across the path of charging enemy cavalry. The caltrop was shaped so that no matter how it fell, three of the spikes formed a stable base, while the fourth thrust up into the air. Unable to see the caltrop, a running horse might bring a foot down on the upthrust

Medieval warhorses were sometimes protected by mail robes, or caparisons, which were draped over their bodies.

spike, impaling or splitting a hoof. The result was a lamed horse.

Whenever practical, a knight had at least one replacement horse on hand during combat. Thus, during one battle the fifteenth-century Spanish knight Pero Niño was able to continue mounted despite having a horse mortally wounded under him:

> Pero Niño felt his horse weaken beneath him; and he looked and saw that it had lost much blood and could no longer bear him. . . . Then he turned the head of his horse, that had reached the end of its forces [reserves], towards his own men. . . . The horse came of a good stock; although strength failed it by reason of the great blows and wounds that it had received, its courage did not fail, and it got its master out of this pass [situation]. Before the horse fell, a page brought up another, and a moment later the brave horse rolled dead to the ground, its entrails [intestines] coming out of its belly.[10]

Saddling Up

The saddle for the warhorse was made from wood, which was held together with glue and rivets. The back of the saddle projected up, to keep the knight from being pushed off the rear of his horse by a blow from lance or sword. Sheepskin, leather, or velvet covered the wood. This covering kept the saddle wood from rotting by preventing the horse's sweat from reaching the frame.

The stirrups were so long that the knight rode almost straight-legged, as though he were standing rather than sitting in the saddle. As military historians David Edge and John Miles Paddock remark, "standing in the saddle . . . enabled [the knight] to use it as a fighting platform, both to take his weight and also to hold him securely in place while delivering or receiving blows."[11]

Decorated saddles were common, and gold and silver designs were particularly popular: King Richard I the Lion-Heart of England had two golden lions on his saddle. Embroidery also ornamented the reins.

A Matter of Identity

In battle, Richard's golden lions identified him to friend and foe alike. Such distinguishing marks were quite common from the twelfth century on. Since medieval knights did not wear uniforms, they needed a way of telling friend from enemy in a fight. Closed helmets obscured the wearer's entire face and even with the open helmet, the mail coif hid so much of the face that early on, according to Walter Clifford Meller, "knights in battle . . . [mistook] their enemies for friends."[12]

To prevent confusion, each knight adopted a unique set of signs, pictures, and colors, whose overall design was his coat of arms. Because these devices were passed from generation to generation, a knight's coat of arms became that of his family.

The creation, display, and regulation of coats of arms are all parts of heraldry. To guarantee the uniqueness of each coat of arms, medieval kings set up official agencies called colleges of arms, which had sole authority in each kingdom to grant a knight permission to claim a specific design for his coat of arms.

The Coat of Arms

The coat of arms had several elements, of which the most important was the shield. Indeed, the shield is the only part of some coats of arms.

To make sure that coats of arms were unique to each knight and his heirs, medieval kings appointed a King of Arms to issue these devices. In this 1450 proclamation, quoted in Maurice Keen's *Chivalry*, John Smert, the King of Arms for England, grants a coat of arms to Edmond Mylle.

"John Smert alias . . . King of the Arms of the Kingdom of England salutes and humbly recommends himself to all present. . . . Reason ordains [commands] that men of virtue and noble courage shall have the reward of renown for their merits, and not just in their own persons in this mortal and transitory life, but in such a way that after their day the issue of their bodies [their descendants] shall in all places be held in honor . . . by means of certain marks and insignia of honor. . . . That is to say by blazon [coat of arms], helm, and crest; so that by their example others shall strive the harder to spend their days in deeds of arms and other virtuous works. . . . Edmond Mylle has long time followed the career of arms and . . . has borne [carried] himself so valiantly and honorably . . . [that] I have devised . . . the following blazon, helm, and crest: to wit, a shield of . . . *sable* [black] and *argent* [silver] charged with [portraying] three bears rampant [standing erect] . . . chained *or* [gold] the chains thrown [wrapped] around them; and the crest upon the helmet a bear sable similarly chained *or* upon a torce [wreath] of *or* and *gules* [red] . . . for him and his heirs to have, hold, use, possess, and clothe themselves with forever."

A fourteenth-century coat of arms belonging to a Knight of the Order of the Golden Fleece.

The surface, or field, of a medieval coat of arms was decorated with geometric shapes or figures called charges.

Two sets of colors were used to shade the field and its charges. Thus, although several coats of arms, for example, featured a single diagonal bar, different color combinations distinguished one from another. Both charges and fields used two sets of colors. The first set of colors consisted of the metallic hues: *or* (gold) and *argent* (silver). In the second set were *sable* (black), *azure* (blue), *gules* (red), *vert* (green), *tenné* (orange), and *purpure* (purple).

Because a coat of arms belonged to a family, symbols, called cadency marks, were added to the field to distinguish between father and sons. The eldest son's cadency mark was a label (a narrow horizontal band, with usually three pendants), while the second son's was a crescent, and the third son's a star. There were nine such marks in all.

The shield design was almost always reproduced on a knight's surcoat, and it could also be placed on a cloth, or mantle, that hung from the back of the helmet. The helmet also carried another element of the coat of arms, the crest, whose animal or bird was painted in colors specific to a particular family. A wreath made from a gold or silver cord was a third part of the coat of arms and twisted around the brim of the helmet. The final element of the coat of arms was a motto, that is, a short phrase or saying: a personal war cry, perhaps, a play on the family name, or a moral sentiment.

On the shield's surface, or field, appeared geometric shapes or figures, called charges. Some of the earliest coats of arms had very simple designs, such as a single bar or a cross. The bar was placed so that it ran across the shield's top or middle, up and down the shield's center, or diagonally across the field. Sometimes it was bent to form an upside-down "V." Later designs became more complicated, including multiple bars. Eventually, designs incorporated various creatures and objects from angels to chess pieces to animals and plants, both real and imaginary.

The financial investment in a knight's gear and his horses was matched by an investment in time. It was no short or easy matter to master the use of weapons, to become accustomed to moving and fighting in armor, and to learn to ride and guide a horse of war. Indeed, the training took years, and the work was hard, sometimes, brutal.

The Training of the Knight

Becoming a knight took years of training, during which a young man learned how to fight, ride, and behave in a proper, knightly manner. The knight in training had to be the son of a knight, a requirement dictated by law in all western and central European kingdoms. The road to knighthood started for the candidate when he was a young boy and did not end until he was out of his teens.

The Early Years

During his first few years, a knight's son was raised and instructed by his nurse, his mother, and the other women of his father's household. He was taught how to behave, with particular emphasis on courtesy, since knights were expected to have good manners—at least toward members of their own social class.

The boy's first knightly training came when he was given a pony at age four or five. From this time on, he would spend a great deal of time learning to ride and look after horses.

Page Boy

Soon the young boy, sometimes at five, but more frequently at seven or eight, was sent from home to begin formal training for knighthood. He went to live and serve in the household of his father's lord or of the king. There he became a page, a knight's apprentice.

The page's uniform was a knee-length shirt, called a tunic, to which was added a short cape fastened with a gold clasp or

During their first few years, knights' sons were raised and instructed by their mothers, their nurses, and other women of the household.

brooch. His legs were covered with hose in winter, bare in summer. Over close-cut hair, the page wore a leather cap, trimmed with fur in the winter.

Life as a Page

In his new home, the young page continued his lessons in proper behavior and horsemanship. The household chaplain gave the boy religious instruction, and in rare cases, might teach a child to read, although generally not to write.

A page's main duties were to run errands and to help with household chores. Some of these chores were to wait upon the lord at meals and at bedtime. The page learned obedience by being obliged to appear promptly when called and patience by learn-ing to wait when there was nothing for him to do.

Starting with a blunt or wooden sword, the page began picking up the basics of swordsmanship. This process was often painful, since a missed stroke often was rewarded by a hard, bruising thump from an instructor's sword.

The Hunt

Hunting was another important part of the page's training. His confrontation with often dangerous and unpredictable animals, such as wild boars, forced him to develop the skills necessary to survive in battle: the abilities to improvise and use his wits to counter danger. He became a capable outdoorsman and could identify and follow an animal by its

Hunting helped pages learn how to travel through dense forests without getting lost, to identify and track animals, and to use weaponry effectively.

tracks and other traces. He also learned how to travel through dense forest without getting lost.

Hunting was also a way to test a page's weapons skill. Boars and other large animals were hunted both mounted and on foot with spears. And, although he would not use it in battle, the page learned how to shoot a bow, which required a steady hand and a good eye. The abilities learned with spears and bows and arrows helped in mastering other weapons, particularly the lance.

A Page Becomes a Squire

At the same time that the page was being trained in horsemanship, swordsmanship, and hunting, he was learning other hard lessons of medieval life. Military historians A. Vesey B. Norman and Don Pottinger write that "it was a harsh age; beatings must have been common, and rough discipline among the pages would have been maintained by the older ones. Slowly the boy would learn . . . self-discipline, the most important of all military virtues."[13]

At fourteen, a page who made good progress in this rough-and-tumble training program could look forward to taking the next step toward knighthood, that is, becoming a squire. He was raised up to squire in a religious ceremony. Accompanied by his parents, carrying large candles, the young candidate appeared before his lord's chaplain. He was then presented with a sword and belt, both of which had been blessed by the priest.

Although the former page still had much training before him, he was now considered a fighting man. He was allowed to put on silver spurs, to wear a knight's helmet, and to carry a shield displaying his family's coat of arms.

A Squire's Responsibilities

The squire continued his apprenticeship but now under the guidance of a single knight, one of those living in the castle of his father's lord. Acting as both companion and servant to his knight, the squire found himself with numerous duties. He helped his master to put on his armor, and cleaned it after use. Currying horses and cleaning out the stables also fell to the squire.

He further served his master at meals, even carving the knight's meat for him, and he dressed the knight in the morning and undressed him at night. After bringing his

The duties of a squire included helping his master don armor.

master a final cup of spiced wine at bedtime, the squire took up his post of sleeping across the knight's doorway. The thirteenth-century Spanish knight, Ramón Llull, wrote that to be under the authority of a knight was the best way for a would-be knight to learn about the nature of that authority: "the son of a knight . . . should learn how to serve, before he becomes a lord, or he would not understand how noble is the authority of a knight. Therefore, every man who wishes to become a knight, should learn how to serve, arm, and equip one."[14]

Hard Training

Under the eye of his master, the squire continued his military training, working on his swordsmanship and building his strength by running, jumping, and wrestling. He also spent hours working out with the heavy weapons of knighthood until he could wield them for long periods at a time without tiring. He also learned to leap into his horse's saddle without using the stirrups and to guide the horse with knees and heels. And, he continued to hunt regularly with spear and bow.

Along with the sword, the squire trained with the lance. At first, he rode at a shield fixed on a fence so that he could learn to hold the long weapon steady and hit the unmoving shield squarely with the lance tip.

Later, he moved on to the quintain, the chief training tool for the lance. Mounted on an upright post, a pivoting crossbar had a shield at one end and a heavy sack at the other. The squire would tilt, that is, ride at full gallop with lance leveled, aiming for the shield. When the shield was hit, the force of the blow would send the crossbar spinning and the heavy sack would sweep swiftly around. If the squire did not duck quickly enough—and beginners never did—he was knocked out of the saddle. Eventually, his reflexes were honed to quick response.

Readying for War

The squire's weapons training eventually moved from drills to practice skirmishes with other squires of the household. Like a knight, he would also take part whenever possible in the mock combats of tournaments. As one anonymous medieval writer remarked, "A youth must have seen his blood flow and felt his teeth crack under the blow of his adversary and have been thrown to the ground twenty times . . . ; thus will he be able to face real war with the hope of victory."[15]

Facing actual combat was a real possibility for a squire because when his master went to war so did the squire. Recently promoted squires did not participate in battle; they did not yet have the necessary military skills. However, older squires who were sufficiently advanced in the use of sword, lance, and other weapons rode and fought in battle alongside their master knights.

Chivalry

A squire's education included more than the skills of war. He also had to become familiar with chivalry, the code of conduct of knights on and off the battlefield. Chivalry, like chevalier, the French term for knight, is a word that comes from *cheval* the French word for horse. Chivalry began to take form in the eleventh century, and by the middle of the thirteenth its major principles were to be found in manuals of knighthood, two of the best known being the Spanish knight

The Squire

Both the following fifteenth-century documents, John Harding's poem "A Squire's Training" and an untitled, anonymous piece from the *Harleian Manuscripts*, reprinted respectively in *The Black Prince* by Richard Phillipson Dunn-Pattison and *Those Who Fought*, edited by Peter Speed, describe the life of the squire.

"At fourteen years, . . . [the squire] shall
  go to the fields
To hunt the deer, and catch one with
  boldness.
For to hunt and slay deer, and see them
  bleed,
Such boldness teaches him courage,
And also in his wits to take heed
so that in council he takes advantage of
  them.

[He learns] to wage war,
To joust and ride, and castles to attack,
To all skirmishes goes, so as to make certain of his courage,

And at night stands watch for perils;
And every day his skills he tests
In feats of arms with some of the men
His strength to prove, and what he might do
If we were in jeopardy
If war happened, so that by necessity
He might use weapons in every way to defend:
Thus should he learn his priorities
His weapons are to be at hand at all times."

"[The squires] eat in the hall. . . . Each of them takes at night half a gallon of ale. For the winter season, each takes two . . . candles and one faggot [bundle of wood]. . . .

Each of them is allowed one honest servant. . . . If any of them be ill, he takes two loaves, two messes [servings] of the principal meat, and one gallon of ale for each day. They also have all the year, straw for their beds.

The squires . . . talk of chronicles of kings, . . . harps, sing[ing], or . . . martial arts."

Ramón Llull's *Book of the Order of Chivalry* (1276) and the French knight Geoffroi de Charny's *Book of Chivalry* (ca. 1350).

In part, chivalry was a means of emphasizing the qualities needed to be a good warrior and a good vassal. Chivalry dictated that to face the rigors of combat, a knight had to be brave, while a good vassal must display honor and loyalty. On the battlefield, a knight was expected to match his lord's courage. Therefore, he would continue to fight, whatever the odds or the danger, until his lord ordered a retreat. Honor required that a knight always obey his feudal lord and always keep his word, while loyalty consisted of never betraying his lord in any matter, large or small.

In addition to these virtues, the ideal chivalric knight was devoutly religious and had a desire for justice. According to Llull:

The duty of the knight is to defend the holy Catholic faith. . . . Our glorious God has chosen knights to vanquish . . . unbelievers who strive to destroy Holy Church by force of arms. . . . Knights should uphold justice, for as it is the duty of judges to judge, it is the duty of knights to protect

According to fourteenth-century French knight Geoffroi de Charny's *Book of Chivalry*, knights should avoid physical comforts because they would otherwise dodge the necessary hardships of knighthood. This lesson is one that both pages and squires would have learned in their years of training.

"Men of worth [good knights] tell you that you must in no way indulge in too great fondness for pampering your body. . . . Too great a tendency to cosset [pamper] the body is against all good. . . . If you have this bad tendency . . . , you will want to go to sleep early and wake up late, . . . and the longer you sleep the less time you have to acquire knowledge and to learn something of value. . . . Those who want to attain high honor . . . have often to go to sleep late and rise early, . . . and this helps them achieve physical fitness and honor. . . . [Pampering] also requires . . . soft beds, and if these are lacking, such men's backs and ribs ache so much that they can do nothing at all. . . . The contrary is true of those who seek honor, for . . . they have poor beds and many a time they sleep without beds . . . and with their clothes on. . . . In addition, to sustain these wretched men's bodies, . . . they have to be provided with the best food and wine. . . . And because of this gluttony, they dread the hardship associated with deeds of arms. . . . Those who go in search of this high honor . . . have no regard for and do not indulge in such pleasures, but drink and eat whatever small amount they find and are satisfied. . . . Wretched men . . . in winter . . . are wrapped in furs . . . , and in summer are lightly clad . . . ; otherwise they cannot survive because of their decadent habits."

Knights and other noblemen participate in a feast.

them from violence. If a knight could become learned in the law, none would be better suited to hold the office of judge.[16]

Courtliness

In part, chivalry also laid out ways in which knights should behave toward other nobles, both men and women. Known as courtliness, the possession of social graces added a sophistication and refinement that smoothed the rough edges of a man whose business it was to fight and kill other men. Courtliness was not extended to serfs, peasants, and townspeople, whom many knights treated harshly.

Thus, in preparation for becoming a courtly knight, a squire was expected to act and speak courteously. He further had to be able to amuse guests by chatting pleasantly and entertainingly, by playing chess and other games, and by singing, dancing, and performing music. He also learned to dress well in the current fashion. As Charny notes in *Book of Chivalry*, "the finest games and pastimes . . . [are] conversation, dancing, and singing . . . , while maintaining in word and deed and in all places . . . honor."[17]

A Failure of Ideals

Most squires, and indeed most knights, fell short of achieving the chivalric ideal. A knight who could live his life fully by the chivalric code was indeed a perfect knight. There were few of them. In reality, neither chivalry nor fealty (faithfulness to one's lord) kept powerful, ambitious knights from attacking and grabbing off sections of their neighbors' land or even that of their lords. Further, knights were not always brave, nor

Knights, such as the one depicted on this fourteenth-century stained glass window, were expected to be devoutly religious.

were many of them devout, just, or courtly. Charny condemns such knights for their "dishonest . . . behavior," claiming that they "behave like cowards and traitors. . . . They have no desire to live a valiant and good life."[18]

Still, some knights did their best to live according to the chivalric code. For example, Charny himself not only wrote his *Book of Chivalry*, he was noted for actually being a chivalrous knight. And in the best tradition of chivalry, in 1356, Charny was killed defending his lord, King Jean II of France, in the Battle of Poitiers. According to the fourteenth-century writer Jean Froissart, "among other dead men . . . who fought that day by the king . . . valiantly . . . [was] the lord of Charny, on whom was great press [fierce attack], because he bore the

The chivalric knight was expected to show bravery and honor, and always remain faithful to his lord.

sovereign banner [flag] of the king."[19] Upon such chivalric examples, squires were expected to model themselves.

From Squire to Knight

Around the age of twenty-one, a squire was considered old enough to take on the responsibilities and duties of knighthood. Still, before he could take the knightly vow, he had to demonstrate to an examining knight that he had the physical strength, courage, and weapons skill for the job. Additionally, he had to show that he was of good character. Finally, he had to be able to afford a knighthood.

By no means did all squires become knights. Some were judged unworthy because they lacked the skills and qualities

necessary for knighthood. Most, however, were not accepted because they did not have the land or the money needed to equip and maintain themselves as knights. Many, therefore, remained squires for their entire lives. Historian Frances Gies elaborates:

In both England and France the economic pressures . . . gave birth to a new social category, the sons of knights who were entitled by birth to knighthood, but who now remained squires (in France . . . squires multiplied until they were more numerous than knights). In one district [of France] . . . , all eligible men were knights in 1230, but by 1270 there were four *damoiseaux* [squires] to one knight. Some men died as *damoiseaux* but transmitted their nobility to their sons, who might become knights or remain *damoiseaux*.[20]

These lifelong squires often hired themselves out to knights for service of a year or so.

The Ceremony of Knighthood

If a squire satisfied the examining knight regarding his fitness to be a knight, he then prepared himself for the elaborate ceremony of knighting, known as dubbing. This ceremony, whose chief elements were in place by the late twelfth century, was generally scheduled for one of the major church holidays. The spring feasts of Easter and Pentecost were favored. The setting was one of the great lords' castles, perhaps even the king's residence.

On the day before he was dubbed, the knight-to-be joined other candidates in confessing his sins. Then, along with his fellows, he cut his hair short. Both medieval men and women saw their hair as their crowning glory, so to cut it off was to humble oneself before God.

Purifying Body and Soul

The next step for the candidates was a bath, in which they symbolically washed away their sins. For the remainder of the day, the young

Knighting Ceremony

Jean of Tours left this contemporary account, quoted in *Life in a Medieval Castle* by Joseph and Frances Gies, of the 1128 knighting of Geoffrey of Anjou by the English king Henry I. The dubbing ceremony was not yet the solemn affair seen later in the century. The importance of Geoffrey's family is evident from the richness of his clothing and equipment.

"When [Geoffrey] entered the inner chamber of the king's hall, surrounded by his knights and those of the king . . . , the king went to meet him, and . . . led him to a seat. . . . All that day was spent in joyful celebration. At the first dawn of the next day, a bath was prepared. . . . After bathing, Geoffrey donned a linen undergarment, a tunic of cloth of gold, a purple robe, silk stockings, and shoes ornamented with golden lions; his attendants, who were being initiated into knighthood with him, also put on gold and purple. . . . [Geoffrey] left the chamber to appear in public. Horses and arms were brought and distributed. A Spanish horse of wonderful beauty was provided for Geoffrey, swifter than the flight of birds. He was then armed with a corselet [shirt] of double-woven mail . . . , and shod with iron boots of the same double mesh; golden spurs were girded on; a shield with golden lions was hung around his neck; a helmet was placed on his head gleaming with many precious stones, and which no sword could pierce or mar; a spear of ash tipped with iron was provided; and finally from the royal treasury was brought an ancient sword. . . . That day, dedicated to the honor of the newly made knights, was spent entirely in warlike games."

The fourteenth-century French knight Geoffroi de Charny in his *Book of Chivalry* had this advice for those who would be successful knights.

"The truest and most perfect form [of knighthood] . . . exists. . . . in those who . . . with their understanding . . . like to hear and listen to men of prowess [ability] talk of military deeds, and to see men-at-arms [knights] with their weapons and armor and enjoy looking at the mounts and chargers; and as they increase in years, so they increase in prowess and in skill in the art of arms in peace and in war; and . . . the desire in their hearts grows ever greater to ride horses and to bear arms. . . . They do not seek advice nor do they believe anyone who wants to counsel them against bearing arms. . . . And they themselves, through their great zeal [enthusiasm] and determination, learn the true way to practice the military arts until they on every occasion, know how to strive toward the most honorable course of action, whether in relation to deeds of arms or in relation to other forms of behavior appropriate to their rank. Then they reflect on, inform themselves, and inquire how to conduct themselves . . . without waiting for admonitions [warnings] or exhortations [urgings]. Thus it seems that such men have made a good reputation for themselves through their own efforts; in this way they double the good to be found in them, when from their own instinct and the will for good . . . , they know what is right and [do not] spare . . . themselves . . . to achieve it."

men lay upon beds, a reminder that they would rest in heaven if they lived up to the ideals of knighthood. To keep in mind what those ideals were, each recited over and over the rules of chivalry.

In the evening, according to Charny's *Book of Chivalry:*

knights . . . come to the beds to dress those to be knighted; the stuff in which they dress them . . . should be . . . new, white, clean material, signifying that they should all from henceforth keep themselves pure and free from sin. Then the knights should robe them in red tunics, signifying that they are pledged to shed their blood to defend and maintain the faith of Our Lord and the rights of the Holy Church and all the other just rights [set out in the code of chivalry]. . . . Then the knights bring black hose . . . ; this signifies . . . that from earth they [the candidates] have come and to earth they must return [in death] . . . ; they know not at what hour [they will die]; therefore they should put all pride beneath their feet. Then the knights bring them white belts . . . , signifying that they should surround their bodies with chastity and purity . . . [and] red cloaks . . . as a sign of great humility.[21]

After the knights finished dressing the candidates, they led them to the castle chapel for the vigil at arms. Each knight-to-be placed his weapons on the altar to be blessed. Then he prayed, keeping in mind that his weapons were to be used only in God's service.

Dubbed a Knight

In the morning came the greatest moment in the life of a knight, his dubbing. First, the candidate knights attended a church service, and then they either remained in the chapel or paraded outside to stand on carpets or platforms. In both cases, they faced a crowd of nobles, knights, relatives, and general curiosity seekers. Amid blowing trumpets, knights buckled onto each candidate his sword, the edges of which reminded the new knight that justice and loyalty were joined, while other knights fastened to the young men's heels the golden spurs.

Finally, there followed the accolade, delivered by the senior knight present. The accolade was either an open-handed blow to the neck, shoulder, or head that sometimes knocked a young knight to the ground or a light touch on the shoulder with a sword. According to an anonymous thirteenth-century authority on knighthood, the accolade was delivered "in remembrance of Him [God] who ordained you and dubbed you knight."[22]

Celebrating Knighthood

Each new knight now received a gift. Frequently, this gift was a warhorse in full harness, a gift of either the knight's father or his father's lord. After mounting their horses, the young

The dubbing ceremony ended with an accolade, which could be a light touch on the shoulder with a sword or an open-handed blow to the neck, shoulder, or head.

Squires who exhibited great courage in combat sometimes received the accolade on the battlefield.

warriors took up lance and shield and rode against one or more quintains. They might also take part in a mock battle celebrating their knighthoods. That night, they would attend a feast at which they received golden collars.

Although this elaborate ceremony was the most customary way of being dubbed a knight, it was not the only way. Some squires were made knights with far less fanfare. Squires who had performed bravely and well in combat often received the accolade on the battlefield, standing among the dead and dying. At other times, a lord would find himself short of knights on the eve of battle, and since only knights could lead troops, he would rush several squires through a very brief dubbing ceremony. Both occasions were opportunities for poor squires, who under normal circumstances could not afford to become knights.

These young warriors were now ready for battle. Some had already been to war as squires with their masters; others had yet to see real combat. But, as a rule, they were all anxious to find a battlefield, and not just for glory. The battlefield was the major source of income for many knights.

Campaign and Battle

War was the ultimate test of a knight's military training. His skill with a lance and a sword and his ability to meet the physical demands of medieval combat determined whether he could survive on the battlefield.

Knights saw nothing wrong with war. Rather, they regarded it as a natural, and desirable, part of human existence. The fourteenth-century writer Honoré de Bonet described war as "good and virtuous; for war . . . seeks nothing other than to set wrong right . . . in accordance with Scripture."[23]

Honor and Glory

Knights also saw war as desirable because it offered a path to honor and glory. Individual glory was so eagerly sought by most knights

War was a natural part of existence to the medieval knight, who regarded it as an opportunity to gain honor and glory.

that its pursuit often overruled common sense. Experienced veterans, instead of opposing an attack against overwhelming odds, often enthusiastically favored such an action, if it presented a great opportunity for personal glory.

In 1167, for instance, Gerard of Ridfort, a knight of much experience, but in search of glory, led a hundred knights in a direct attack against a much larger force. Gerard and only two others survived the battle. In 1244 honor and glory again drove an army of knights to leave the safety of a strong position during a campaign in the Near East to rush out to grapple with the enemy. This rash attack, too, led to the death of most of the participating knights.

Courage and Cowardice

The impulsive aggression of knights also arose from a need to prove their courage. In urging his knights to the attack, Gerard had shamed those who argued that the odds were too great by calling them cowards.

A knight's courage did not come from a lack of fear, but rather from the fear of dishonor from cowardice. Writing in the fourteenth century, the French knight Geoffroi de Charny observed that:

> You will often be afraid when you see your enemies charging you, their lances in rest to strike you and their swords drawn to attack you. Bolts and arrows fly at you. . . . Now you see men slaying each other, fleeing, dying, . . . while your friends' corpses lie before you. Your horses, though, are not dead, and you could escape. . . . If you remain, you will be honored for ever more. If you escape, you will dishonor yourself.[24]

The fear of dishonor was very great, for a knight who fled from battle risked losing his knighthood. Even if he remained a knight, his reputation was ruined for the rest of his life. No action on his part could repair the damage. In 1098, during battle, Count Stephen of Blois panicked and fled and became, as one contemporary put it, "an object of contempt to . . . everyone, and was continually reproached because he had fled disgracefully."[25] Even though Stephen took part in other campaigns, finally dying in battle, he never regained his reputation.

Making a Living

In addition to honor and glory, many knights had a more practical reason for going to war: money. War was the only livelihood some knights had. Thus their entire income depended upon their fighting in one conflict after another.

There were numerous mercenary knights during the Middle Ages. Many younger sons of knights had no fiefs to inherit, for these grants went to the oldest son. After a younger son's training, he was sent out into the world supplied with armor, weapons, and horses. Beyond that, he was penniless, and if he could not win a fief of his own, he could make money only by hiring out to fight in various wars.

Even knights with fiefs could find themselves forced to turn mercenary to make a living. Many fiefs were not large enough to produce the income needed by a knight and his family, and as happens in every age, even those with profitable holdings sometimes fell on hard times.

A Knight's Wages

Knights had several ways of making money through war. The first was simply being paid

In the fourteenth century, the French knight Geoffroi de Charny explained in his *Book of Chivalry* that a good knight learns war by going to war.

"[Knights] want to observe and find out how to set up an expedition to attack and fight one's enemies, and to observe the deployment of light horsemen, the deployment of men-at-arms [knights] and foot soldiers, and the best way to advance on a fine attack and to make a safe and honorable withdrawal, when it is time to do so. And when they have observed that, then they will not be content until they have been present at and learned about the defense of castles and walled towns; how they can be held, guarded, and provisioned [supplied] against both enemy attack and siege, and against all advances against them which can be made. . . . And they still do not want to give up at this point, even though they have achieved great honor in this form of practice of arms [defense]; they always want to learn more because they hear people talk about how one can lay siege to walled towns and castles. Then they do their best to seek out the places where such sieges are going on. And when they come there, they take great pleasure in seeing how a siege is set up to surround the town or castle, how . . . to block the way out for the besieged, and to exert more pressure on them, . . . [and] how to mount an attack on the walls, to climb up on ladders, and to pierce the walls and to enter and take by force. . . . And the more these men see and themselves perform . . . , the more it seems to them . . . that they are still only at the beginning."

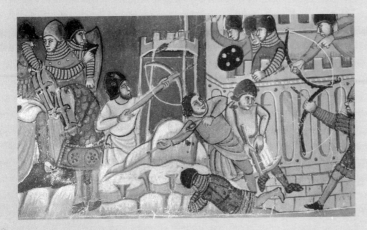

A fourteenth-century manuscript illumination of a siege on a castle.

by another noble to fight. Occasionally, knightly mercenaries banded together into companies, and the group as a whole sold their services.

Whether as an individual or as part of a company, knights were paid by the day, with a knight receiving about twice as much as a squire. Although these knights, too, had to have their own armor, weapons, and horses, it became common practice for employers to replace or pay for mercenaries' horses killed in battle.

Loot and Prisoners

In addition to his regular pay, a knight added to his income by looting. Both knights and common soldiers took anything and everything of value that they came across on the campaign trail. They routinely stripped the dead and dying of valuables and scavenged any possessions left behind by a defeated foe.

A knight also earned money by ransoming other knights captured in battle. Until the eleventh century, prisoners, whether noble or common, were frequently killed out of hand. However, although the practice of killing captured enemy infantry and archers continued, knights were generally spared, so that they or their families could pay a handsome ransom for their release.

Paying Ransom

A wealthy prisoner could bring the equivalent of thousands, even hundreds of thousands, in current dollars. But even a modest ransom could support a poor knight for six months to a year. Additionally, the personal property—armor, weapons, horses, clothing, and baggage—of a captured knight belonged to the captor.

In England and France, a captive knight was treated like a guest. After giving his word of honor not to escape, the prisoner not only lived with his captor until ransomed, but also joined him in hunting, feasting, and gaming. Captured knights in Germany and Spain, on the other hand, were treated less well, often finding themselves chained to a wall in some castle dungeon.

However kind or harsh his treatment, a ransomed knight frequently found himself in financial trouble. Between his ransom sum and his forfeited equipment, a captured knight could lose everything he owned. And if

Knights supplemented their regular pay by looting anything of value they came across on the campaign trail.

he were not already on the mercenary circuit, he soon would be.

Staying Home

By no means were all knights eager for battle. Many of those with large enough incomes from their holdings spent only brief periods of time in combat and in some cases never went to war at all. Norman and Pottinger explain:

The idea that the . . . medieval aristocracy constantly rode about in full armor is entirely wrong. Many of the gentry . . . occupied themselves with the management of their estates, interesting themselves actively in farm management. . . . The demands of local government gave them little time for military exercises. . . . Such knights might pass their whole life without putting on the armor they inherited from their father. . . . Even the sword was not worn in civil life except by travellers.[26]

If called upon, a fief-holding knight was, of course, obligated to fight a certain number of days a year—the period generally was limited to forty days. But it was usual for knights whose interests lay more with their estates than on the battlefield to pay their lord a fee, called scutage, to avoid military service. As explained in a twelfth-century English document, scutage was "a certain sum . . . paid from . . . [a] knight's fee [fief] . . . to provide wages for . . . soldiers."[27]

This arrangement satisfied both the reluctant warrior and his lord. The former did not have to ride off to war, and the latter bought himself an army of mercenaries, who did as they were ordered and stayed as long as they were paid, rather than leaving the day before a battle because their service time of forty days had run out.

On the War Trail

Knights who went to war found it a hard business. When out campaigning, a knight generally rode most of each day and sometimes much of the night with few breaks. He might be accompanied by servants and a pack train of horses carrying supplies, among which was a tent. Or, there might just be the knight and his squire with no tent and little to protect them from cold, heat, or rain.

In his fifteenth-century biography of the Spanish knight Pero Niño, Gutierre Díaz de Gómez comments that the food on campaign was frequently bad: "moldy bread or biscuit, meat cooked or uncooked; today enough to eat and tomorrow nothing."[28] The knight got drinking water from ponds and rivers. Occasionally, he also carried wine in a small cask or a wineskin.

Being Wounded

The hard business of war, of course, always included the possibility of dying or being

An illumination from a manuscript page depicts a wounded soldier being transported from the battlefield. The wounds received in battle by medieval knights often led to death.

Healing the Wounded

These excerpts, the first from *Those Who Fought*, edited by Peter Speed, and the second from *The Unconquered Knight* by Gutierre Díaz de Gómez, describe the limited medical treatments available for wounded knights.

"The leech [doctor] whom he [Baldwin of Boulogne, a French knight and one of the leaders of the First Crusade] summoned feared . . . lest the cataplasm [herb paste] outwardly applied might film over the wound, which . . . had pierced deep into the prince's body. He feared . . . , while the skin grew smooth over the wound, it might rankle inwardly with . . . putrid matter [become infected]. . . . [Thus he decided] how perilous it would have been for . . . [Baldwin] if the lips of the wound had become united before the matter had been drawn forth and the bottom [of the wound] had grown together."

"The best surgeons of Seville [in Spain] met to examine . . . [Don Pero Niño's] wound. They found it so serious that several desired to cut off the foot, for there was danger of death [from infection]; and if the foot were cut off, there was a chance of life. . . . [Instead] the surgeons decided to cauterize [to burn] the wound with a burning iron [rod], and they told him that once matters were thus, he must bear this operation, and they would see if they could heal him.

They heated an iron . . . white hot. . . . The glowing iron . . . [was] moved . . . from one end of the wound to the other. Without stopping, . . . a second [rod] like it . . . [was] applied. . . . Thenceforward his wound was well dressed, and it pleased God that each day it should mend."

wounded, for no amount of armor, even plate, could provide perfect protection. As in wars of any period, being wounded was more common than being killed.

Wounds could, and did, lead to death, however. Many knights stayed on the battlefield after having received numerous injuries. Some even had arrows impaling arms, shoulders, and legs. Now and then, a wounded knight bled to death because he had refused to stop fighting to attend to his wounds.

Treating the Wounded

Wounded men who survived the battle faced the grim reality of medieval medical care, or more accurately, the lack thereof. Medical knowledge during this period was almost nonexistent, and doctors had few good ways of treating injured knights. They had nothing with which to anesthetize their patients during the painful business of removing arrows or digging mail links out of a wound. Nor did they have any way to control pain.

A common and frequently deadly problem was infection, since antibiotics and other bactericidal drugs were far in the future. If an infection had not burrowed deep into the body, it could be treated by the application of a red-hot iron. Such treatment, hard on the patient, might or might not kill the infecting agent. For deep wounds that became infected, no medical remedy existed, and the patient either recovered on his own or died of blood poisoning.

The Raiders

Knights took part in few full-scale battles because such combat was not a usual feature of medieval warfare. Certainly pitched battles were fought, and several, such as Crécy and Agincourt during the Hundred Years' War between England and France, became famous.

But raiding and sieges were much more customary, and the average knight's military career was very like that of the famous twelfth-century English knight William Marshall. In his entire career, which spanned some fifty years, Marshall took part in only two battles, but he participated in seventeen sieges and countless small raids.

During a war, a knight could expect to take part in many hit-and-run raids, aimed at destroying crops, peasant and serf dwellings, and even whole villages. The goal of such raids was to ruin the economic base of the enemy lord. Frequently, raiding knights cold-bloodedly targeted the common folk who worked the land. The raiders killed men, women, and children by putting them to the sword, hanging them, and even burning them alive in their homes.

The brutality of these massacres might seem contrary to chivalry. However, the chivalric code did not extend to behavior toward peasants and serfs whom the elite-minded knights regarded as no different from the livestock they also destroyed. Scholar Matthew Strickland writes that, to knights, "attacks on the peasantry formed the logical extension of . . . economic warfare. . . . An opponent sought to deprive . . . [an enemy lord] of his workforce."[29]

The Siege

When not raiding during war, knights were laying siege to castles and fortified towns, often bottling up enemy forces who might otherwise interfere with the raids. In the process,

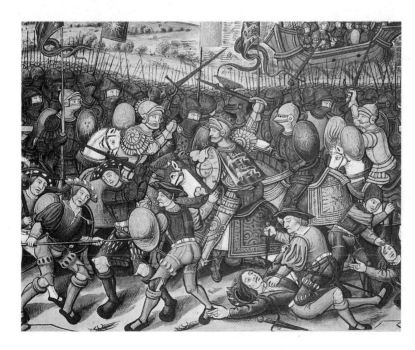

Raids and sieges were more common in medieval warfare than pitched battles such as the Battle of Crécy depicted here.

the besiegers tried to capture these castles and towns, as well as the knights and soldiers defending them.

It was easy to throw a ring of troops around a castle and town and keep anyone from entering or leaving. Taking these fortresses was another matter, since the defenders were often well supplied with food and water and were protected by tall, thick stone walls.

The besieging army's task was either to break down part of the walls or to climb up and over them. Generally, a direct attack was preceded by a long period of bombardment with catapults, heavy-duty machines that threw rocks and barrels of boiling oil, and by assaults on walls and gates with battering rams.

While the attackers were busy with siege engines and battering rams, they were under

Medieval knights and soldiers often attempted to capture castles by besieging them, thereby keeping anyone from entering or leaving the castle.

This anonymous account, taken from *Life in the Middle Ages*, edited by George Gordon Coulton, tells of the 1315 siege by Scottish forces of the English town of Carlisle. The affair quickly turned into a battle between Scot and city siege engines.

"The king of Scotland assembled all his forces and came to Carlisle, where he compassed the city round about [surrounded the city] and besieged it. . . . On each day of the siege they [the Scots] made an assault against one of the three city gates. . . . We cast upon them from the wall javelins and arrows and stones. . . . On the fifth day . . . they set up an engine . . . [that] threw great stones without intermission [stop] against the wall and the Calden gate; yet with all this they did little or no harm to the townspeople, save only that they slew one man. . . . We had seven or eight such engines in the city . . . , which wrought [caused] much terror among the besiegers. . . . In the meanwhile the Scots set up a great Belfry, like a tower, which far overtopped the city walls; whereupon the city carpenters, upon one tower against which this belfry must have been set if it had been brought up to the wall, built another tower of wood that overtopped that belfry. But the Scottish engine never came against the wall; for when men dragged it on its wheels over the wet and miry [muddy] ground, there it stuck fast with its own weight, nor could they draw it forward or harm us. . . . On the eleventh day, . . . the Scots retired . . . to their own land, leaving behind all their engines of war."

fire from the castle or town. The defenders shot arrows and crossbow bolts at the soldiers operating the catapults and swinging the battering rams.

Siege Combat

Unlike raids, with their fast, hard rides, which ended in a burst of frantic action, sieges were mostly dull, static affairs for the beseigers. During most of a siege, the invading knights had little to do because the work of breaking down the walls was carried out by siege specialists and soldiers, none of whom were knights. The defending knights were equally idle, and both sets of noble opponents quickly grew bored.

To pass the time, the knights on one side would challenge their peers on the other side to a siege combat, a generally nonlethal test of arms. Siege combats were sometimes fought with both parties separated by the barriers, the wall of a castle or town surrounding the main gate. If this wall was short enough, a defending knight standing inside on a catwalk set just below the wall's top and a besieger standing outside at the foot of the barriers could duel each other with lances or spears, much as though they were using very long swords. Neither knight, however, could actually touch the other. Fourteenth-century chronicler Jean Froissart described one such siege combat:

[The besiegers] gave their horses to the pages and servants, and marched in a compact body, each knight and squire with his spear in hand. . . . When they were come as far as they wished, they halted for a short time, and then advanced . . . to begin the action. They were gallantly received; and, I believe, had the two parties been on the plain [outside the barriers], many more bold actions would have taken place than it was possible to find an opportunity for where they were; for the barriers [gate] being closely shut, prevented them from touching each other. . . . So every man had his match; and when they were fatigued or heated, they retired and other fresh knights and squires renewed the skirmish.[30]

Close-Quarter Attack

Not all sieges ended in an attack by the besieging army. The besieging commander might work out a surrender agreement with the besieged. Or he might decide that the target was too difficult to capture. Or he and his army might simply run short on supplies and have to retreat.

The sieges that did end in an attack finally gave the knights on both sides the combat that they so desired. The besieging knights would compete with one another to lead an assault, since being among the first to enter a town or castle was a great honor. The early arrivals also would be among the first to fight against the defending knights.

If the siege engineers succeeded in breaking through a wall, the knights would lead an attack through the break. Sometimes, they could ride their horses through this gap. If not, they made the assault on foot, being followed by an army of foot soldiers. Many of these were mercenaries, while others were permanent employees of the attacking lord.

Medieval knights employed tall, wheeled structures called siege towers to scale the walls of a castle.

Scaling the Walls

When a defender's walls proved too strong and well built to be brought down, knights used tall ladders or siege towers to gain access. The ladder route was particularly dangerous, for the defenders poured boiling water or oil or dropped rocks or hot cinders onto the climbing men. Some of the climbers carried long poles that ended in large hooks, with which they could snag a defender, pulling him from the walls. The defenders, in turn, had their own poles, with which they pushed the scaling ladders away from the walls or knocked climbers off.

Siege towers were tall, wheeled structures that were pushed up against the besieged walls. When such a tower was in place, attacking knights standing on an upper platform rushed directly onto the walls.

Invaders Versus Defenders

If a few attacking knights could reach the top of the wall and hold off the defending knights and soldiers, their numbers soon were swelled by reinforcements. From the walls, the attacking party fought its way down stairs to the ground level.

The invaders' goal was to open one or more of the gates so that they could let in the bulk of their army. The defender knights' job was to overwhelm the invaders and thus keep most of the enemy forces outside and harmless. Often whether a castle or town fell was determined by who won the battle of the gates.

A captured castle or town could expect to be looted by invading knights and soldiers, after which it became the property of the invaders' lord or employer. Captive knights were ransomed. However, defending soldiers,

The outcomes of large wars were usually decided by the full-scale battles fought by knights and soldiers.

if not killed outright, were mutilated: most frequently the victors cut off each man's right foot.

On the Battlefield

Most of the wars fought during the Middle Ages were small, local affairs between rival nobles. Upon occasion, much larger conflicts broke out, such as the periodic warfare between France and England. These large wars had their share of raids and sieges, but they also set the stage for full-scale battles fought by armies of knights and soldiers. It was these battles that often decided the winner of the war.

For battle, knights organized themselves into groups. The smallest of these units, a banner group, contained ten to forty knights. Several of these units made up a squadron. And three or four squadrons formed a battle group. Part of the battle group was kept in reserve to be used as reinforcements if necessary.

According to Malcolm Vale, "these mounted troops kept close order, endured enemy attack without retaliating, [and] charged in [a] line." However, discipline as is found in a modern army did not exist, and "a battle might dissolve into a series of hand-to-hand encounters, where the taking of prisoners took precedence over destruction of the enemy."[31]

Battle tactics were fairly simple. The knights of each side formed a line opposite that of their foes. Then each line charged at the other with lances at the ready. The two lines crashed into each other, with some knights going down, pierced by lances. Others broke their lances in unsuccessful attempts to unhorse an enemy.

Discarding the lances, the knights then drew their swords, battle-axes, or maces, and either as part of their group or as individuals fought hand-to-hand duels with the opposing knights. In the heat of battle, a knight often forgot about ransom money and pressed the fight to the death.

Songs of War

The twelfth-century knight and troubadour Bertrand de Born captured his class's love of bloody battle and plunder in these two songs, reprinted in *Life in a Medieval Castle* by Joseph and Frances Gies.

"I love to see,
Amid the meadows, tents and pavilions
    spread out,
And it gives me great joy to see
Drawn up on the field
Knights and horses in battle array,
And it delights me when the scouts
Scatter people and herds in their path.

Maces, swords, helms of different colors,
Shields that will be riven [split] and shat-
    tered
When the fight begins;
Many vassals struck down together,
And the horses of the dead and wounded
Roving at random.

I tell you I find no such savor [gusto]
In food, or in wine, or in sleep,
As in hearing the shout, "On! On!"
From both sides, and the neighing of
    steeds
That have lost their riders."

"We are going to have some fun.
For the barons will make much of us.
To the soldier's pay will be added loot:
Trumpet, drums, flags and pennons
    [streamers],
Standards of horses white and black—
This is what we shall shortly see.
And it will be a happy day,
For we shall seize the usurer's [money-
    lender's] goods,
And pack animals will no longer pass in
    safety,
Or the burgher [townsman] journey with-
    out fear,
Or the merchant on his way to France,
But the [fighting] man full of courage will
    be rich."

Infantry Attack

Until the fourteenth century, enemy foot soldiers posed only a limited threat to knights: far more dangerous were men armed with crossbows. After 1300, however, knights also had to face ground troops armed with longbows, weapons capable of bringing down knights and horses. Later in the same century, foot soldiers began carrying pikes, eighteen-foot-long spears that could impale a horse or its rider.

The halberd also proved deadly to the knight. Eight feet in length, this weapon had a heavy cleaverlike blade mounted on a wooden shaft. The back of the blade had a curved spike. A soldier armed with a halberd used its curved spike to hook a passing knight and drag him from his horse. Then with a powerful downward swing of the blade, the soldier split the knight's helmet and sliced through the man's skull down to the teeth, killing him instantly.

Knights themselves sometimes acted as infantry against both other knights and foot soldiers. On occasion, particularly when the ground was too broken or rough for a cavalry charge, they dismounted and fought on foot. Having ridden to the battleground, the knights were fresher than enemy infantry, who had marched to battle.

Feudal Europe was not the only region offering war and reward. In the Balkans, knights served as mercenaries in the Byzan-

Wielding weapons such as the halberd, the infantry became more powerful during the fourteenth century.

tine Empire, and in Spain, they hired out to various Muslim rulers. But the greatest campaigns, and among the most profitable in terms of both glory and money, were in the Near East during the Crusades.

CHAPTER 4

Crusades and Knightly Orders

During the late Middle Ages, unlike the first five centuries of the period, warfare in Europe was far from constant. Most conflicts were short and limited in scope—generally no more than picking off some property of a neighbor—and periods of peace were common.

Knights who looked to war for glory, adventure, or income had a hard time of it during times of peace. Representative of these unemployed warriors was the English knight and mercenary Sir John Hawkwood, who upon being wished peace by two friars, replied, "May the Lord take away your alms [donated money]. . . . Do you not know I live by war and peace would be my undo-

ing?"[32] Thus, many knights welcomed the Crusades, the holy wars of the twelfth and thirteenth centuries that sent thousands of the mounted warriors to fight in the Near East.

Call to Holy War

In 1095 Pope Urban II called for a military expedition to free Palestine and Jerusalem from the Seljuk Turks, who were Muslims. The pope promised western knights who participated in the enterprises, which became known as the First Crusade, that if killed, their sins would be pardoned and they would

Pope Urban II (standing) proposes the First Crusade, a military expedition to free Palestine and Jerusalem from the Seljuk Turks.

A fifteenth-century painting of crusader knights capturing Jerusalem in 1099.

be heavenbound. If they survived, however, they could share in the wealth of the region.

Christians responded enthusiastically to the pontiff's appeal, and knights gathered from all over western Europe, with the bulk coming from France. The Crusade offered a church-approved way to both express religious devotion and seek material gain. Knights saw the war as an opportunity to gain riches through plunder and conquest, while simultaneously defending Christianity. Many shared the sentiments of the twelfth-century monk Guibert of Nogent, who wrote that:

> God in our time has introduced the holy war so that the knighthood . . . might have a new way to win salvation. They [knights] need not choose the life of a monk and abandon the world . . . , but can obtain God's grace through their own profession, in their accustomed freedom and secular [nonreligious] dress.[33]

Each knight had to take a vow before he was considered a crusader. In this vow, he swore to reach Jerusalem, so that he could pray in front of the Holy Sepulchre, the shrine believed to have been the tomb of Jesus. He was given a cross to wear on the front of his surcoat. Those who returned from the Crusade were to signify their success by placing the cross on their backs.

A Hard, Brutal War

Some four thousand crusading knights and twenty-six thousand soldiers reached Muslim-held land in 1097 when they entered Asia Minor. The crusaders spent the next two years in hard campaigning. They suffered from heat, thirst, hunger, and disease, and they laid siege to cities and fought pitched battles. They succeeded in taking Jerusalem in 1099.

The First Crusade Sets Out

In this eyewitness account, excerpted in *A Source Book of Medieval History*, edited by Frederic Austin Ogg, Fulcher of Chartres describes the emotion-laden departure of the First Crusade, whose knights would be gone from home for years.

"Oh, how great was the grief, how deep the sighs, what weeping . . . among the friends, when the husband left the wife so dear to him, his children also. . . . And yet in spite of the floods of tears which those who remained shed for their friends about to depart, . . . the latter did not suffer their courage to fail, and, out of love for the Lord, in no way hesitated to leave all that they had held most precious, believing without doubt that they would gain a hundred-fold in receiving the recompense [reward] which God had promised to those who love Him.

Then the husband confided to the wife the time of his return and assured her that, if he lived, . . . he would return to her. He commended her to the Lord, gave her a kiss, and, weeping, promised to return. But the latter, who feared that she would never see him again, overcome with grief, was unable to stand, fell as if lifeless to the ground, and wept over her dear one whom she was losing in life, as if he were already dead. He, then, as if he had no pity (nevertheless he was filled with pity) and was not moved by the grief of his friends (and yet he was secretly moved), departed with a firm purpose."

The crusaders slaughtered much of the Muslim population, as they had in other cities captured by them during the war before moving on to Jerusalem. They also satisfied their need for loot and discharged their crusader vow, as one anonymous crusader wrote:

Our men rushed around the whole city, seizing gold and silver, horses and mules, and houses full of all sorts of goods, and they all came rejoicing and weeping from excess of gladness to worship at the Sepulchre of our Saviour Jesus, and there they fulfilled their vows to him.[34]

The Crusader States

Many of the victorious crusaders, wealthy now from their share of the spoils, returned home. Others remained and carved up their conquests into four states, the largest of which was the Kingdom of Jerusalem. Within fifty years, however, Muslim armies began retaking crusader holdings, capturing the first in 1144 and the last in 1291. During this period, seven other Crusades unsuccessfully attempted to reconquer that lost territory.

While they lasted, the crusader states were rich booty for European knights, who ran these territories along traditional feudal lines. The king of Jerusalem was at the top; below him were the princes of the other three states, followed by the highest ranking knights, and then the ordinary knights.

The crusaders quickly divided the land up into fiefs and constructed castles, often better designed and built than those found in Europe. Some vassals lived on and worked their estates just as they had back home. Others preferred to be absentee landlords, spending their time in the cities.

The rewards of victory were great. The knights found themselves surrounded by luxuries unheard of in Europe. Their houses, which were taken over from wealthy Muslims or modeled upon existing Near Eastern homes, had running water, rich carpeting and wall hangings, and fine art work decorating each room. The victors soon discarded their heavy wool clothing for lighter, brightly colored silks and cottons.

The Military Orders

Not all knights attracted to the crusader states came to share in the wealth. Some came solely out of religious duty. They took seriously the chivalric code's call to defend the church and to wage war against non-Christians.

These religiously minded knights banded together in organizations known as military orders. The original purpose of the orders was to serve crusaders and Christian pilgrims.

A fourteenth-century manuscript illumination depicting crusader knights in Jerusalem after its fall. Many crusaders remained in Jerusalem after its capture.

The anonymous author of this account, excerpted in *Medieval History: A Source Book*, edited by Donald A. White, details the struggle of knights of the First Crusade to capture the Muslim city of Marra in late 1098.

"Our leaders . . . caused a wooden siege-tower to be built. . . . On the top storey stood many knights . . . and underneath were armed knights who pushed the tower up to the city wall. . . . The pagans [Muslims] . . . made an engine by which they threw great stones upon our siege-tower so that they nearly killed our knights. . . . [The siege-tower] was higher than all the walls of the city. Our knights who were on the upper storey . . . threw great stones down upon those who stood on the city wall, and struck them upon their shields, so that shield and man fell backward into the city, and the man was killed. While they [the knights] were doing this, others . . . tried to pull the enemy towards them with lances and hooks of iron. Thus they fought until the evening. . . .

On the other side of the city, our knights were . . . putting up scaling-ladders against the city wall. . . . Geoffrey of Lastours was the first to get up the ladder on to the wall . . . ; the ladder broke at once under the weight of the crowd who followed him, but nevertheless he and some others succeeded in reaching the top of the wall . . . [and] cleared a space around them on the wall. . . . The Saracens [Muslims] attacked them. . . . While those very gallant men . . . were resisting the enemy attack, others protected by the siege-tower were undermining the defenses [walls] of the city. . . . Our men all entered the city. . . . The Franks [crusaders] stayed in the city for one month."

Some escorted pilgrims from western Europe to Jerusalem, while others took care of sick or stranded Christian travelers and warriors. Each order also took a hand in the military defense of the crusader states against Muslim raids.

The Soldier Monks

At the head of each order was a master, who was selected through a complicated procedure involving both an election and the drawing of lots. The master was served by an assistant, the seneschal. There were other officials as well: a supreme military commander, a treasurer, and a supply officer.

All the member knights were like monks, even calling themselves brethren, or brothers. Like a monk, each member, no matter what his rank within the organization, took a vow of chastity and poverty. These orders interpeted "chastity" very strictly: they did not mean for their members simply to avoid sexual relations, but to forego all relations with any women. One order, the Knights Templars, even insisted that "none of you [member knights] may presume to kiss a woman, be it . . . mother, sister, [or] aunt."[35] The orders also commanded that members should have no personal possession, since their weapons, armor, horses, and clothing were supplied by the organization. The brother knights also slept and ate together.

The military orders came to control many of the best castles in the region and fielded the finest and most disciplined fighting forces in the crusader states. In battle, the knights of these orders were well organized and fiercely pressed the attack. They neither asked for nor gave mercy. Thus, instead of taking prisoners, they killed any survivors of vanquished fighting forces.

The Knights Templars

The first of the military orders, and the last to leave the Holy Land, was the Order of the Temple of Solomon, which was founded in 1119 and whose members were called Knights Templars. The organization took its name from the location of its headquarters, near the site of the Temple of Solomon in Jerusalem, which had been destroyed some fifteen hundred years earlier, rebuilt, and destroyed again in A.D. 70.

The Templars began as an escort service for pilgrims. For this purpose, they had a fleet of ships, which they also used to engage in trade, carrying such goods as silks, dyes, and porcelain. Even more importantly, the Templars' ships transported money back and forth between Europe and the Kingdom of

Knights Templars, such as the one depicted on this twelfth-century fresco, were originally escorts for pilgrims.

Jerusalem. This financial operation developed into their most prominent enterprise, and the Templars became bankers.

The trade and banking businesses made the order wealthy and powerful in both Europe and the Near East and seemed to some outsiders to be contradictory to the order's vow of poverty. Still, as Desmond Seward writes, making money and monastic living often went hand in hand:

> Such activities hardly [seem to] harmonize with the name of Poor Knights. . . . The Templars owned no individual property, but in common seemed anxious to possess everything. . . . Nevertheless their life was as ascetic [lacking in comfort and material goods] as ever. Purely contemplative orders [monasteries] were no stranger to high finance. . . . [Certain] techniques of agriculture brought great wealth to . . . [some] monks—the entire wool crop of many English abbeys was often sold for years ahead.[36]

Nonetheless, great wealth and power often create great enemies. One of the Templars' clients and enemies was the French king Philip IV, to whom the order made a number of large loans. Like many European rulers who borrowed money, Philip was always short of cash and always had difficulty paying back his loans. One solution he hit on to ease his economic troubles was to get rid of his creditors. First, he expelled all Italian and Jewish bankers and confiscated their property.

Rules of Conduct

The Knights Templars had an extensive set of rules, regulating every aspect of Templar life. This passage, taken from *The Rule of the Templars*, sets down in detail how a knight of the order was to be outfitted.

"138. Each knight brother . . . should have three horses and one squire; . . . a fourth horse and a second squire, if he have them, are at the discretion of the Master [of the order]; and they should have a . . . ration of barley for their horses; a hauberk, iron hose, a helmet, . . . a sword, a shield, a lance, a Turkish mace, . . . mail shoes, and three knives: a dagger, a bread-knife and a pocketknife. They may have . . . two shirts, two pairs of breeches [pants] and two pairs of hose; and a small belt which they tie over the shirt. And all the brothers should sleep [dressed] thus. . . .

139. And each should have . . . three pieces of bed linen: . . . a bag in which to put straw [for a mattress], a sheet and a light blanket . . . ; also a rug [heavy blanket] . . . to cover his bed or his coat of mail when he rides out; . . . the rug should be white or black or striped. . . .

140. And each may have a cloth [napkin] for eating and another with which to wash his head; . . . and a blanket to cover his horses. . . . And he should have a cauldron [large kettle] for cooking. . . . And he may have three saddlebags: one for the brother and two for the squires; and two cups for drinking; . . . a bowl . . . and a spoon. And he may have one cloth cap and one felt hat; [and] a tent."

The French king Philip IV took over the funds and property of the Knights Templars after falsely accusing the order of heresy.

Then, in 1307, after the Templars had relocated from the Near East to Europe, Philip set out to destroy the order. Arresting sixty knights on the basis of false charges, he tortured them and had them convicted of heresy. Leaders of the order, including the master, were burned at the stake, and the organization was abolished by the pope.

Philip took over all the Templars' funds and property in his kingdom. Equally eager to be rid of Templar debt, the king of England and the Holy Roman Emperor quickly followed the French monarch's example and confiscated the order's holdings in their lands.

The Hospitallers

The Order of the Hospital of St. John of Jerusalem, was the second major military order. Like the Templars, it was headquartered

Knights of the Order of the Hospital of St. John, or Hospitallers, cared for sick or wounded pilgrims and crusaders.

in Jerusalem. The knights of this order, known as Hospitallers, cared for sick or wounded pilgrims and crusaders. The order grew wealthy through donations from grateful patients, some of whom became Hospitallers themselves.

With the end of the crusader states, the order moved its hospital operations first to Cyprus and then Rhodes. From the latter island base, they became a major medieval naval power in the western Mediterranean.

The Hospitallers and the Templars were bitter rivals, and to distinguish between the two orders, Templars began wearing a red cross on white and the Hospitallers a white cross on black. The two normally took opposite sides in any political dispute within the crusader states, and their rivalry even led each order into alliances with Muslim rulers against the other. On occasion, the Hospitallers and the Templars actually fought each other on the battlefield.

Other Orders

In addition to the Templars and the Hospitallers, Jerusalem had other military orders, among which were the Order of St. Lazarus, the Knights of Our Lady of Montjoie, and the Teutonic Order. St. Lazarus was also a hospital order, its specialty being leper hospitals: all its member knights had leprosy or one of the other skin diseases common in the region at the time. The Lazarus Knights, as they were known, wore black, to which eventually was added a green cross.

Like the Templars, both the Knights of Our Lady of Montjoie and the Teutonic Order, also called the Teutonic Knights, escorted and protected pilgrims. The Montjoie knights wore a white cloak with a red and white cross, and part of their revenues went to ransoming crusaders and pilgrims captured by the Muslims. However, the order did not prosper and ended by merging with the Templars.

Originally, the Teutonic Order, whose knights wore a white cloak with a black cross, offered its services only to Germans, but it came to extend its protection to all Christians. After leaving the Near East, the Teutonic Knights focused on eastern Europe, where the order eventually conquered and converted to Christianity the Prussians living in what would become Poland.

Orders of Chivalry

The Teutonic Knights had a tradition of singling out a few knights who had distinguished themselves in combat as participants in one of the order's crusading expeditions into eastern Europe. Heralded as models of chivalry, these men were seated at a special table during a feast in their honor. At the end of the banquet, each honored knight received a shoulder badge on which was written in gold "honor conquers all." The whole ceremony was labeled a Table of Honor. Maurice Keen notes that a Table of Honor "encouraged the pursuit of martial distinction . . . , and it responded to a need on the part of chivalrous society for a measure of formal recognition of its high purposes."[37]

To satisfy this need for recognition, orders of chivalry popped up all over Europe beginning in the fourteenth century. These knightly orders were not religious in nature. Rather, nomination and initiation were often controlled by kings and other rulers. Among these chivalric societies were England's Order of the Garter, France's Order of the Star and Order of St. Michael, and the Holy Roman Empire's Order of the Golden Buckle.

The 1430 charter for the duke of Burgundy's Order of the Golden Fleece, with its goals of encouraging and recognizing chivalric behavior, was typical of these organizations:

> [The order is] to honor and increase the noble order of chivalry; and also for the three following reasons: firstly, to honor older knights whose noble . . . deeds are worthy of recognition; secondly that those who are now strong and able-bodied, and exercise deeds appropriate to chivalry . . . , may have cause to continue them even better than before; and thirdly, that knights . . . who see this order worn . . . may be moved to noble deeds themselves and lead such a life that . . . they will deserve to be chosen to wear the said order.[38]

Entering an Order

A knight gained entry to a chivalric order by performing some worthy and heroic—and by definition, chivalrous—deed on the battlefield.

At a formal ceremony, sometimes in public, sometimes in private, the honored knight took an oath to support the other members of his order, as well as his sovereign. He also swore to follow the society's rules, knowing that failure to do so, or being judged guilty of unknightly conduct, could result in expulsion.

Once enrolled in an order, the knight had the right to wear its insignia, or badge. The badge of the Order of the Garter, for instance, was a band worn around the arm or leg.

Knightly Women

Some of the orders of chivalry admitted women to their ranks. Meller writes that "they were 'honorary members,' and as such had certain privileges" but they "were certainly not admitted to knighthood,"[39] which was restricted to men.

Even though women could not be knighted, they were known to put on armor and take up swords when the battle for a castle or town grew desperate, as happened during a twelfth-century attack by Muslims on the Spanish town of Tortosa. And, in 1429, Joan of Arc, dressed in armor and carrying a sword, led French troops to victory over the English at Orléans. Although Joan's family was made noble after her death, she never had a title.

Joan of Arc and the female defenders of Tortosa were rare exceptions, however. As a rule, a woman's connection with knighthood was as mother, wife, sister, or daughter of a knight. A wife of a knight sometimes had a title that was a feminized version of her husband's. Thus, in France, she was a chevaleresse and in Spain, a cavallera.

Many orders of chivalry, such as the Knights of the Golden Fleece shown here, were formed in the fourteenth century.

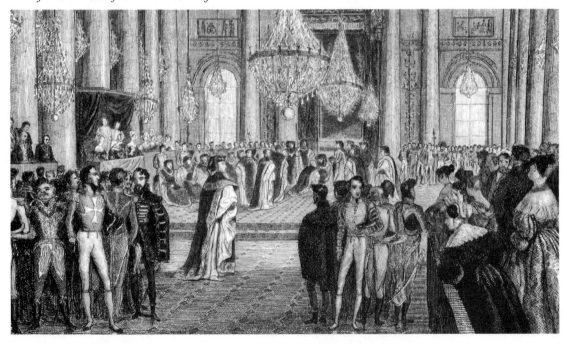

Joan of Arc led French troops to victory over the English at Orléans in 1429.

A Woman's Coat of Arms

Noble women also had the right to their family's coat of arms. A woman, however, did not display her arms on a shield, but rather on a smaller, diamond-shaped object, known as a lozenge. Nor did she have a crest or a mantle.

A knight whose parents had individual coats of arms bore a shield with both designs on it. Such a shield was divided into four sections, with two devoted to the father's coat of arms and two to the mother's. If the knight married a woman with a coat of arms, hers would be added to both of his on their son's

Crusades and Knightly Orders **65**

shield. Such heraldic divisions continued down the generations, resulting in some very complex shield patterns.

In War and Peace

The wife of a knight frequently had responsibilities beyond the raising of children and other traditional domestic matters. In many marriages, it was the wife who took over the management of the knight's fief when he was off at war. Sometimes, she continued this supervision even after the knight's return.

More often, however, a knight coming home from war picked up his peacetime duties as a fief holder. Nevertheless, even in peace, the knight kept in mind his primary occupation as a warrior and found ways to keep his battle skills sharp and ready.

Manor and Tournament

All wars, even the longest, finally end. Knights who lacked fiefs moved on looking for new conflicts in which to enlist. The remainder went home to peacetime responsibilities and pleasures.

The Manor

The home to which a knight returned might be a castle on a huge estate, or it might be a modest house sitting on a few acres of land. For a household knight, or retainer, home was a room or barracks in his lord's holding.

Most knights, however, came back to a manor house on an average-sized estate. The house, made of wood or stone, was the largest structure on the manor, its two or three stories overshadowing the surrounding farm buildings and peasant huts. At the house's center was the great hall, which was as high as the house because it was not divided into stories. Here estate business was conducted, meals eaten, and guests entertained. Extending from opposite ends of the great hall were two wings, one for the servants and the other for family and guests. Next to the manor house was often the local church, which doubled as storehouse, courthouse, and prison.

The knight's land, stretching out from the manor house, was four hundred to six hundred acres of farmland, pastures, and woodlands. Included in the fief were also the one and two-room huts of serfs and freeborn peasants and perhaps even a village or two.

The knight's personal household was often quite large. In addition to his wife and children, it contained relatives who lived with him, his squire, any retainers, and the servants required by members of the household.

Country Gentleman

The knight set himself apart from the serfs and peasants who made up the bulk of the manor's population, even though his peacetime concerns were the same as theirs. He wanted to see that fields were planted and harvested on time and that animals received the necessary care until slaughtered. Indeed, the knight's most important peacetime duty was to see that food production on the estate remained as high as possible.

In part, production had to be high to ensure that the knight's lord received his assigned share of the fief's income. In part, the knight was concerned because his own prosperity depended upon the success of each harvest. Thus, whenever possible, he arranged for new varieties of seeds and new breeding stock to be introduced to his manor.

Still, the knight did not farm himself. As the fourteenth-century chronicler Honoré de Bonet observed, "a knight must not cultivate the soil or tend vines . . . , and he must not be a shepherd. . . . The reason is, that the knight must not be tempted to forsake arms." In his thirteenth-century *Book of the Order of*

The knight depended on the peasants and serfs who lived on his manor to provide him with a successful harvest.

Chivalry, the Spanish knight Ramón Llull wrote that "a knight should lead a life in keeping with his status, exercising himself with hunting and enjoying those things which others provide him with [by] their labors."[40]

Going Hunting

Even a knight who involved himself deeply in the workings of his fief made time for hunting, which was among the favorite pastimes of the warrior nobility. On a hunt, the knight was accompanied by members of his household and any guests staying with him. The hunting party was attended by servants, a professional tracker and woodsman, and dog handlers.

Knights hunted almost any kind of edible animal or bird, for hunting was an important source of food for the knightly household. Generally, in the summer, the prey was male deer, and in the winter, wild boar. Both animals were dangerous. A male deer could impale a man with its heavy, pronged antlers, but the boar, an intelligent animal with razor-sharp tusks, was the more formidable opponent. It was not unusual for one or more people to be killed on a boar hunt.

The dogs used on the hunt were prized possessions of a knight and were the responsibility of their handlers, known as dogboys, who lived with their charges. To hunt a stag, the dogboys brought a bloodhound, as well as several greyhounds and smaller hounds called brachets. The bloodhound tracked the deer, while the other hounds chased it down. The dogs used to hunt boar were large and powerful and resembled modern German shepherds.

The Chase

The summer hunt was a festive occasion, which normally was preceded by a picnic lunch. Afterward, the knight and his companions, mounted on horses and, armed with either lances or bows and arrows, followed the howling dogs until they cornered a stag. One of the hunters then completed the kill with a lance thrust or an arrow shot.

There was no picnic before a boar hunt. The hunters, armed again with lances or bows, had to catch the animal out of its den because no amount of noise or dogs would cause it to leave its burrow. Bringing down a boar in the open country was difficult because the animal moved rapidly and unpredictably.

During the summer hunt, knights and their companions armed themselves with lances or bows and followed hunting dogs until they cornered a stag.

Falcons

The type of hunting that most excited any knight was falconry, in which falcons, or hawks, were used to catch other birds flying out of range of a bow. In large part, the attraction of falconry was the skill that this form of hunting required. Holy Roman Emperor Frederick II, an enthusiastic falconer, wrote in 1250 that:

By the proper use of falconry, birds of prey are taught to accept the company of humans, to fly after quarry and to behave exactly as they would in the wild. Anyone who merely plays at hunting can hold dogs in leash or let them go. But in falconry, no beginner can hunt so easily, either by carrying his birds or by setting them at their prey. Falcons . . . become clumsy or impossible to manage, if they are handled badly. . . . Without a teacher of experience, and without constant practice . . . , no one, noble or common, can obtain even an elementary knowledge of falconry.[41]

If learning to hunt with falcons was difficult, so was training them, for it took an expert falconer a long time and much patience to prepare a bird for hunting. This labor-intensive training meant that falcons were very expensive and a true luxury. But, if a knight could afford more than one bird, he saw to it that his wife and oldest children each had one.

Training a Falcon

This thirteenth-century account, reprinted in *Those Who Fought*, edited by Peter Speed, describes the initial training of a hunting falcon. In the first step, known as seeling, the bird's eyelids were sewn together (later the stitches would be removed).

"After the seeled falcon has been placed on the wrist, she should . . . [be] carried around a dark room, alone with her keeper. This must go on for a day and a night. . . . She may be moved from hand to hand and men may take turns to carry her. . . . During all this time, she should not be fed, so that on the second day she is very hungry.

The falconer should now have a chicken leg in his pouch, and should take the bird into the dark, quiet room where she will be more easily persuaded to eat this food for the first time. This precaution may seem unnecessary because the bird is seeled, but her thin eyelids do not keep out the light and she will be reluctant to eat since the daylight reminds her of her life in the wild. . . .

The falconer touches her beak, breast, and feet with it [the chicken leg]. This is done to irritate the bird, so that she will snap at the meat. Then, when she bites it, the taste will please her. . . . Now is the time for the falconer to make a soothing sound. . . . A line from a song will do, . . . and whenever she hears it, she will expect to be fed. . . . In this way, the bird will soon become accustomed to her keeper . . . and not be disturbed by his presence."

The difficulty of training a falcon attracted many knights to falconry.

While hunting, a knight's falcon rode on his glove-protected wrist. This glove, which had the knight's coat of arms on it, was used for no other purpose than carrying the falcon. When the knight spotted a bird to be caught, he gave his wrist a toss, sending the falcon up and after its prey.

According to Joseph Gies and Frances Gies, "a favorite bird shared his master's bedroom and accompanied him daily on his wrist." Knights sometimes even carried them into battle. "Proud, fierce, and temperamental,"[42] the falcon seemed to reflect knightly nature.

Fun and Games

When days were too hot or too cold for hunting, the knight and his household found other sport. Gaming was a popular diversion for any knight. And no game was played more enthu-

siastically than chess, which spread rapidly throughout Europe in the twelfth century. Because of its warlike goal, which must be pursued strategically, the game appealed to knights, who came to associate playing chess with nobility.

Knights also enjoyed dice, a form of backgammon, and on nice days, nine-pin bowling, played under leaves of the manor's orchard. In all these pastimes, including chess, knights almost always wagered on the outcome.

The Troubadours

Another favorite amusement of the knight and his household was provided by periodic visits from traveling entertainers: actors, jugglers, acrobats, and minstrels. Beginning in the twelfth century, many of the minstrels began singing the extremely popular songs composed by a group of poet-songwriters, the troubadours. Occasionally, a troubadour himself might appear at a manor, singing his own songs or hiring a minstrel to do so.

The appeal of troubadour songs for a manor knight was that the composers were generally knights writing about knights. Contemporaries describe these poets in terms used only for knights: thus one was "a good knight and a good warrior," another was "a poor [penniless] knight but clever and well-bred and skilled at arms," while a third was "a courtly man and eloquent."[43]

A majority of these poets were younger sons who had found a way of making a living that did not involve being a mercenary. The successful troubadour found a patron, that is, a wealthy noble who paid the composer a good salary to keep turning out songs. In some cases, patrons, such as the English king Richard I the Lion-Heart, wrote their own troubadour poetry.

Courtly Love

Although some of the troubadours wrote about war and other subjects, their main focus was courtly, or romantic, love. In a courtly love poem, there is a knight, who is in love with a married woman. Although she accepts

The warlike strategy of chess made it the knight's favorite game.

Many an evening for a knight's household ended with singing; the twelfth-century French knight and poet Arnaut Daniel produced some of the most popular songs of the period. This example is found in *The Knight in History* by Frances Gies.

"In this gay, charming air
I will put words so honed [sharpened]
   and pared
That when they've pass beneath
My file, they'll be true [straight] and
   sure
For love at once smooths and gilds [cov-
   ers with gold]
My song, which proceeds from her
Whom Merit guides and sustains.

I continually improve and purify myself,
   for I serve the gentlest lady
In the world and say so openly
I am hers from head to toe,

And even amid cold winds,
The love raining within my heart
Keeps me warm in harshest winter.

I do not want the Empire of Rome,
Nor to be elected Pope, if I
Cannot return to her for whom
My heart burns and cracks;
And if she does not cure my ills
With a kiss before the new year,
She'll kill me and condemn herself.

Yet in spite of the ills I suffer,
I shall not desist [stop] from loving,
Even though I remain in solitude,
For I can still set words to rhyme.
Love makes my lot worse than that
Of a peasant. . . .
I am Arnaut who gathers the wind
And hunts the hare with the ox
And swims against the incoming tide."

his love, she refuses any physical intimacy. Maurice Keen points out that "her acceptance of her admirer's love . . . [means] her acceptance of his amorous [loving] service, not admission to her bed." This service, Keen continues, "was essentially comparable to [like] the . . . faithful service to a lord; indeed it [courtly love] borrowed not a little of its vocabulary from . . . [the] vocabulary of lordship and fealty."[44]

Thus, the knight is the vassal and the woman the lord. Hanging between happiness and despair, he writes her poems and provides other tokens of his love at her command, but can expect no reward be-yond the opportunity to perform his duty faithfully.

Practicing War

The enthusiasm of many knights for the troubadours and courtly love did not lessen their eagerness for war. Certainly, England's Richard the Lion-Heart continued to wage it in both France and the Near East while writing courtly love pieces.

During times of peace, many knights missed the excitement of battle. Further, they were afraid that they were becoming rusty, losing their fighting edge. And knights-for-hire who were unemployed were desperate for money. The answer to all these needs was the tournament, a mock combat that was very popular with knights.

The Tournament

Tournaments had begun in the eleventh century as simple training exercises that allowed knights to practice their fighting techniques. During the next century, however, the affairs grew into full-blown, elaborate spectacles, which could last for days. Only wealthy knights could afford to sponsor these very expensive contests.

A fighting area was set up outside a castle or a town. Surrounding this space, called the lists, were brightly decorated viewing stands and the tents in which the participating knights lived during the tournament. Outside each tent hung a knight's shield. A knight who wished to deliver a challenge rode up to another knight's shield and struck

Richard the Lion-Heart, along with many other knights, did not allow his enthusiasm for courtly love to diminish his zeal for war.

A Tournament

In this account, quoted in *Those Who Fought*, edited by Peter Speed, the fourteenth-century chronicler Jean Froissart describes a tournament near London, as well as the festivities surrounding it.

"On the Sunday . . . , there issued [emerged] from the Tower of London, first threescore [60] coursers [horses], ready for the jousts. . . . Then issued out threescore ladies of honor, . . . richly appareled [clothed] for the jousts; and every lady led a knight with a chain of silver, . . . [and the] knights were appareled to joust. Thus they came riding . . . with a great many trumpeters and other minstrels, and so came to . . . where the queen of England and other ladies . . . were ready . . . to see the jousts, and the king was with the queen.

The jousts . . . commenced . . . and continued till it was dark. Then knights and ladies withdrew. . . . There was goodly dancing in the queen's lodgings in the presence of the king . . . , continuing until it was day.

On the next day, . . . you might have seen in . . . London, squires . . . going about with harness and doing other business of their masters. After noon, King Richard [II] came to the place [of the tournament] all armed, richly appareled, accompanied with dukes, earls, lords and knights . . . , and all were ready to joust.

Then the jousts began. Every man strove to obtain honor. Some were struck down from their horses. . . .

The next day, Tuesday, there were jousts . . . by all manner of squires. . . . On Thursday the king gave a supper to all knights . . . , and the queen to all ladies. . . . On Saturday the king . . . departed from London for Windsor. Then there began great feasts, . . . given by the king."

---

it with his lance. If the challenger hit the shield with the butt of his lance, he wanted a friendly, nonlethal fight, but if he used the point, he was demanding a duel to the death.

Mixing It Up

The start of the tournament was announced with a flourish of trumpets. First referees and judges read out the tournament rules and the fighting records of the participating knights. Then the combats began.

Originally, tournament participants fought with the same weapons they used in war. This practice proved too dangerous, however, and after many knights had been badly wounded or killed, blunt lances and dulled-edge swords began to appear at these affairs. Additionally, special reinforced armor was developed just for tournament use.

The main tournament event was a free-for-all battle featuring most of the attending knights. Mounted on their chargers, the fighters were soon locked in a series of single combats, some of which were challenged against challenger and some just random matchups. Groups of four or five knights occasionally made mutual aid pacts, promising to come to one another's assistance if necessary.

Tournament Ransom

During the mass battle, one end of the lists was left open to give defeated knights an exit through which to retreat. Those in retreat were hotly pursued and frequently captured by their victors, for as in real war, prisoners were taken for ransom. The captive knight normally bought his freedom with his armor or his horse.

Tournament ransoms could be very profitable. The twelfth-century English knight William Marshall and a companion certainly found ransoming good business when, in a two-year period, they collected payoffs from several dozen knights captured during tournaments in France. On his deathbed, William would claim that, in a lifetime of tournaments, "I have captured five hundred knights and have appropriated their arms, horses, and their entire equipment."[45]

The Joust

The most popular tournament event was the joust, a two-man duel on horseback. The two knights, astride their destriers, made their way to the lists, where they squared off facing each other. Military historians Norman and Pottinger describe the scene:

> The jousters charged, passing left side to left side so that the shield was towards the opponent. The lance, the head of which had several points to prevent it from actually piercing the armor, was aimed at the opponent across the horse's neck. Points were scored for knocking a man off his horse and for striking off his helm.

In a joust, a knight earned points for breaking his lance, knocking an opponent off his horse, or striking off his opponent's helm.

Around 1260, to cut down on death and injury associated with tournaments, the English king Henry III issued "The Statutes of Arms," reprinted in *The Statutes of the Realm*.

"It is . . . by our Lord the King commanded, that . . . none be so hardy [bold], who shall go to the Tournament, to have more than three Esquires in Arms [squires] to serve him at the Tournament; and that every Esquire do bear . . . the Arms of his Lord, whom he shall serve that day. . . .

And no Knight or Esquire serving at the Tournament, shall bear a sword pointed, or Dagger pointed, or Staff or Mace, but only a [blunted] broad sword for tourneying. . . .

And if it happen that any . . . knight do go against this statute, that such knight . . . shall lose Horse and Harness, and abide in prison at the pleasure of our Lord Sir Edward the King's son. . . . And the Esquire who shall be found offending against the statute here devised, in any point, shall lose Horse and Harness, and be imprisoned three years. And if any man shall cast a knight to the ground, except they who are armed for their Lord's service [taking part in the tournament], the knight shall have his horse, and the offender shall be punished as the Esquires aforesaid [mentioned above].

And they who shall come to see the tournament, shall not be armed with any manner of armor, and shall bear no sword, or dagger, or staff, or mace, or stone, upon such forfeiture [penalty] as in the case of Esquires aforesaid. And no groom or footman shall bear sword, or dagger, or staff, or stone; and if they be found offending, they shall be imprisoned for seven years."

Breaking a lance also counted, since it could only happen when the blow was struck full on the center of the target so that the point did not glance off.[46]

A fighter lost points if he hit the other knight with the lance shaft instead of the point or wounded the other's horse.

The jousting knights made six to eight passes at each other. If they lost their lances, they continued the fight with swords, battle-axes, or maces. Rarely did these events end without injury to one or both men.

Besides the major combat events, tournaments featured some milder contests. Knights wrestled with each other and competed at dart shooting, as well as lance and stone throwing.

A Bad Reputation

The Catholic Church and many European rulers, such as King Henry III of England, opposed tournaments. Even with blunted weapons and special armor, injury and death were common.

A further strike against the tournament was rioting. When the son of William Marshall was accidentally killed at a tournament, a brawl erupted in which one knight was killed and many others injured. Ten years later, a tournament ended with English participants beating defeated French knights with clubs and sticks.

The church was also concerned because tournaments were famous for overeating, drinking, and lovemaking. Jacques de Vitry, a thirteenth-century French priest, used the affairs to illustrate the seven deadly sins, particularly gluttony and lust:

> [Tournament knights] have the mortal sin . . . of gluttony, since . . . banquets were held, where they spent their time . . . in profuse prodigality [extreme excess]. Lastly comes the sin of lust. Do not Jousters first of all seek to please their mistresses?[47]

However, neither civil nor religious authorities succeeded in shutting down the tournaments. Knights routinely ignored threats of excommunication or seizure of land for the sake of holding and competing in tournaments. Even the brother of Henry III, defied an order banning tournaments.

What civil and church decrees could not do, time did. Medieval knighthood and the Age of Chivalry did not survive the Renaissance, and neither did the tournament.

The End of Chivalry

Even before the Middle Ages ended, around 1500, knighthood was beginning to fade. The knight, who had once been a military necessity, was made obsolete by new weapons and new infantry tactics. Nonetheless, although the warrior elite of the Middle Ages vanished, knighthood survived the changing times and even the death of chivalry.

The Pike and the Cavalry

The military importance of the knight was on the decline by the end of the fourteenth century. The longbow and the crossbow had been the first weapons to pierce the iron shell worn by the knight. However, improvements in armor plate had been sufficient to counter these weapons.

But no improvement in armor could protect the knight from the pike and the gun. In the late 1300s, European infantry began adopting the eighteen-foot-long pike spear and army leaders discovered its potential. If enough foot soldiers stood shoulder to shoulder, each holding a pike, no cavalry in the world, no matter how well armed or armored, could break through this porcupine defense. Knights who tried it impaled their horses, themselves, or both. In the words of the fifteenth-century soldier Jean de Wavrin:

> These pikes make very useful poles for placing a spike . . . against the fearful effects of cavalry . . . , for there is no horse which, if struck in the chest with a pike, will not unfailingly die. . . . Pikemen can also approach and attack cavalry from the side and pierce them right through, nor is there any armor however good that they cannot pierce or break.[48]

Guns and Gunners

The gun was slower in making a difference on the battlefield because early models were big clumsy affairs, difficult to handle and not very accurate. Rain could easily put these primitive firearms out of commission by wetting down the gunpowder or the matches needed to light it.

By the late fifteenth century, however, guns, although far from perfect, were more reliable. During this period, Swiss armies began taking advantage of the pike and the gun, without abandoning the older bow and crossbow. The infantry was divided into nine-man units. Each unit had three pikemen, three gunners, and three archers. The nine soldiers learned to work together, making the best use of their weapons. The pikes could hold off mounted knights, while the archers and gunmen killed or wounded horses and sometimes knights.

The Power of the Infantry

When Swiss armies made up of these small, well-coordinated infantry units fought with

The military dominance of the mounted knight suffered when groups of foot soldiers began to arm themselves with pikes in the late-fourteenth century.

knights, the infantry won and the knights lost. It was not long before other European powers were copying the Swiss army model.

The growing importance of infantry and the decreasing effectiveness of heavy knightly cavalry is seen in the ratio of foot soldiers to knights in the late fifteenth century. Keen writes that "the proportion of infantry to cavalry . . . was nine footmen . . . to one mounted man-at-arms. A hundred years before, the proportion might have been one [foot soldier] to one [knight] or even . . . one to two."[49] The infantry was not only becoming more important than the knights' cavalry, but it was numerically dominating European armies.

Cavalry units continued to be part of armies up until the twentieth century. They became fast, mobile strike forces supporting infantry maneuvers. In addition, mounted scouts were the eyes and ears of armies. The cavalry would not be put completely out of business until the rifle and the machine gun ended their fighting effectiveness and the airplane their spying role.

Chivalry's Indian Summer

The medieval knight and the code of chivalry did not disappear overnight. Tournaments were held well into the sixteenth century. Indeed, King Henry II of France died in one in 1559, and England's Henry VIII was almost killed in a joust. Further, the Renaissance saw the finest, best-crafted, and sturdiest armor ever made, although it still would not stop a pike thrust or a bullet.

During this chivalric Indian summer, the nobility continued knighting itself and speaking about chivalrous actions. Yet, the aristocrats embraced the idea that knighthood should be inherited rather than earned. Barber notes that they "fully adopted . . . the insistence on birth as the great criterion [yardstick for achieving knighthood], while abandoning the knighting ceremony."[50] The only knights who had to earn knighthood would be those who were not born the sons of knights.

The New Knighthood

No matter how many tournaments Renaissance monarchs rode in, or how good the armor was, or how many men called themselves knights, the old knighthood was dead. On the battlefield, permanent standing armies filled with professional soldiers, not hereditary warriors, were the norm. Knights who wished to fight had to join these professional ranks and earn promotion just like any other soldier.

As a class, however, knights moved away from military service. Through the nineteenth century, they remained powerful landowners,

Theodore Roosevelt leads his cavalry into battle during the Spanish-American War. The cavalry continued to be a part of armies until the twentieth century.

The chivalry embraced by medieval knights has been seen as the product of ignorance by some, while others claim it is a lost ideal from a purer time.

dominating the political, economic, and social life around them.

The Importance of Chivalry

As for chivalry, it has had a mixed reception through the centuries. Some have ridiculed it as hopelessly naïve, the product of ignorance and superstition. Others, however, have seen it as a lost ideal from a purer time, or as the English poet, Alfred Lord Tennyson put it, "live pure, speak true, right wrong, follow the King."[51]

Both these views represent extreme positions. In general, medieval knights were practical men who may have been ignorant and superstitious, but hardly naïve. On the other hand, few of them always followed Tennyson's commands, and indeed, too many knights were brutal and callous killers who sought wealth and power. A more balanced and fairer assessment of chivalry and the men who embraced it comes from Matthew Strickland, who writes:

> [Chivalry's] workings were largely restricted to a warrior elite. And of this elite, some, perhaps many, fell short of ideals whose binding power lay in a precarious [shaky] fusion of honor and pragmatism [practicality]. Yet even if not adhered to by all, the development and articulation [vocalization] of such ideals was of profound significance. . . . The emphasis on . . . noble conduct befitting a knight went beyond the raw warrior virtues of courage [and prowess [skill]].[52]

Notes

Introduction: The Coming of the Knight

1. Frances Gies, *The Knight in History*. New York: Harper & Row, 1984, p. 14.
2. Gutierre Díaz de Gómez, *The Unconquered Knight: A Chronicle of the Deeds of Don Pero Niño, Count of Buelna*. Translated and edited by Joan Evans. London: Routledge, 1928, p. 11.
3. Quoted in Peter Speed, ed., *Those Who Fought: An Anthology of Medieval Sources*. New York: Italica Press, 1996, p. 93.

Chapter 1: The Outfitting of the Knight

4. Quoted in Joachim Bumke, *The Concept of Knighthood in the Middle Ages*. Translated by W. T. H. Jackson and Erika Jackson. New York: AMS Press, 1982, p. 22.
5. Stephen Turnbull, *The Book of the Medieval Knight*. London: Arms and Armour Press, 1985, p. 43.
6. Jean Froissart, *Chronicles*. Translated by John Bourchier, Lord Berners, and edited by George Campbell Macaulay. London: Macmillan, 1895, p. 197.
7. Froissart, *Chronicles*, p. 104.
8. "Manual of Arms for the Axe," 1999. Translated by Sydney Anglo. www.thehaca.com.
9. *The Song of Roland*. Translated by William Stanley Merwin. In *Medieval Epics*. New York: Modern Library, 1963, p. 139.
10. Gómez, *The Unconquered Knight*, pp. 195–96.

11. David Edge and John Miles Paddock, *Arms and Armor of the Medieval Knight: An Illustrated History of Weaponry in the Middle Ages*. New York: Crescent Books, 1988, pp. 36–37.
12. Walter Clifford Meller, *A Knight's Life in the Days of Chivalry*. New York: AMS Press, 1924, p. 76.

Chapter 2: The Training of the Knight

13. A. Vesey B. Norman and Don Pottinger, *A History of War and Weapons, 449–1660: English Warfare from the Anglo-Saxons to Oliver Cromwell*. New York: Thomas Y. Crowell, 1996, p. 80.
14. Quoted in Speed, *Those Who Fought*, p. 95.
15. Quoted in Norman and Pottinger, *A History of War and Weapons*, p. 81.
16. Quoted in Speed, *Those Who Fought*, p. 93.
17. Geoffroi de Charny, *Book of Chivalry*. Translated by Richard W. Kaeuper and Elspeth Kennedy. Philadelphia: University of Pennsylvania Press, 1996, p. 113.
18. Charny, *Book of Chivalry*, pp. 177–79.
19. Froissart, *Chronicles*, p. 128.
20. Gies, *The Knight in History*, pp. 102–103.
21. Charny, *Book of Chivalry*, p. 169.
22. Quoted in Gies, *The Knight in History*, p. 85.

Chapter 3: Campaign and Battle

23. Quoted in Richard Barber, *The Knight and Chivalry*. Totowa, NJ: Rowman and Littlefield, 1974, p. 202.
24. Quoted in Speed, *Those Who Fought*, p. 91.

25. Quoted in Matthew Strickland, *War and Chivalry: The Conduct and Perception of War in England and Normandy, 1066–1217*. Cambridge: Cambridge University Press, 1996, p. 122.

26. Norman and Pottinger, *A History of War and Weapons*, pp. 82–83.

27. Quoted in Gies, *The Knight in History*, pp. 100–101.

28. Gómez, *The Unconquered Knight*, p. 13.

29. Strickland, *War and Chivalry*, p. 270.

30. Quoted in Barber, *The Knight and Chivalry*, p. 201.

31. Malcolm Vale, *War and Chivalry*. London: Duckworth, 1981, p. 104.

Chapter 4: Crusades and Knightly Orders

32. Quoted in Maurice Keen, *Chivalry*. New Haven, CT: Yale University Press, 1984, p. 227.

33. Quoted in Richard W. Kaeuper, *Chivalry and Violence in Medieval Europe*. Oxford: Oxford University Press, 1999, p. 69.

34. Quoted in Donald A. White, ed., *Medieval History: A Source Book*. Homewood, IL: Dorsey Press, 1965, p. 372.

35. *The Rule of the Templars: The French Text of the Rule of the Order of the Knights Templar*. Translated by Judith Mary Upton-Ward. Woodbridge, England: Boydell Press, 1992, p. 36.

36. Desmond Seward, *The Monks of War: The Military Religious Orders*. Hamden, CT: Archon Books, 1972, p. 39.

37. Keen, *Chivalry*, p. 179.

38. Quoted in Barber, *The Knight and Chivalry*, p. 307.

39. Meller, *A Knight's Life in the Days of Chivalry*, p. 46.

Chapter 5: Manor and Tournament

40. Quoted in Speed, *Those Who Fought*, p. 95.

41. Quoted in Speed, *Those Who Fought*, p. 118.

42. Joseph Gies and Frances Gies, *Life in a Medieval Castle*. New York: Harper & Row, 1979, p. 128.

43. Quoted in Gies, *The Knight in History*, p. 52.

44. Keen, *Chivalry*, p. 30.

45. Quoted in Kaeuper, *Chivalry and Violence in Medieval Europe*, p. 282.

46. Norman and Pottinger, *A History of War and Weapons*, p. 82.

47. Quoted in Meller, *A Knight's Life in the Days of Chivalry*, p. 142.

Epilogue: The End of Chivalry

48. Quoted in Vale, *War and Chivalry*, p. 114.

49. Keen, *Chivalry*, p. 239.

50. Barber, *The Knight and Chivalry*, p. 27.

51. Quoted in Gies, *The Knight in History*, p. 206.

52. Strickland, *War and Chivalry*, p. 340.

For Further Reading

Books

Timothy L. Biel, *The Age of Feudalism*. San Diego: Lucent Books, 1994. Details the workings of feudalism, the economic and political system of the Middle Ages. Illustrations and a reading list enhance the text.

———, *The Crusades*. San Diego: Lucent Books, 1995. Traces the history of the Crusades, looking at the interactions of the societies that gave birth to them. Additional features include black-and-white illustrations, excerpts from eyewitness accounts, maps, a time line, and additional reading.

Gary L. Blackwood, *Life in a Medieval Castle*. San Diego: Lucent Books, 2000. A fact-filled, lavishly illustrated account of how medieval castles came to be and what it was like to live in one.

Thomas Bulfinch, *The Age of Chivalry* (1858) and *Legends of Charlemagne* (1862). In *Bulfinch's Mythology*. New York: Modern Library, 1993. A lively and readable retelling of the medieval stories about the knights of King Arthur and of a highly fictionalized Charlemagne, the first Holy Roman emperor. The introduction gives useful information about the background of the tales.

James A. Corrick, *The Early Middle Ages*. San Diego: Lucent Books, 1995.

———, *The Late Middle Ages*. San Diego: Lucent Books, 1995. Filled with instructive illustrations, these two books trace the history of Europe from the fall of Rome to the beginning of the Renaissance. Each contains excerpts from period documents, maps, a time line, and a reading list.

John Dunn, *The Spread of Islam*. San Diego: Lucent Books, 1996. A well-illustrated introduction to the history of Islam, its origins and growth. Text is supplemented with excerpts from Arabic and European manuscripts, a time line, a reading list, and maps.

Aryeh Grabois, *Illustrated Encyclopedia of Medieval Civilization*. New York: Octopus, 1980. Several hundred entries provide good, detailed information on medieval terms, people, and events. Many excellent full-page, color photographs enrich the text, as do the very useful map section, time line, and bibliography.

William W. Lace, *The Hundred Years' War*. San Diego: Lucent Books, 1994. An in-depth look at the causes, course, battles, and results of this long-running conflict between medieval England and France.

Donald Matthew, *Atlas of Medieval Europe*. New York: Facts On File, 1983. Filled with good, large, easily read maps in color and well-reproduced photographs, mostly in color. A good commentary with special sections on such subjects as the Catholic Church is supported by a time line and a bibliography arranged by country and topic.

Don Nardo, *Life on a Medieval Pilgrimage*. San Diego: Lucent Books, 1995. Filled with reproductions of period woodcuts, paintings, and drawings, this volume describes the daily lives of religious pilgrims, explaining their goals and motivations.

———, *The Medieval Castle*. San Diego: Lucent Books, 1998. This readable and information-packed account follows the building of a medieval castle. Black-and-white drawings and a reading list accompany the text.

Earle Rice Jr., *Life During the Crusades*. San Diego: Lucent Books, 1998. An informative, well-illustrated description of daily life for both Christians and Muslims during the period of the Crusades.

———, *Life During the Middle Ages*. San Diego: Lucent Books, 1998. A good survey of medieval country and city life; examines social order, religion, families, farming, commerce, war, disease, education, and the arts, particularly architecture.

Internet Sources

Pred S. Bundalo, "Medieval Weapons and Armor," 1997. epsilon.ece.nwu.edu/~pred/medieval. Presents excellent color photographs of armor, including full suits, helmets, breastplates, and weapons, showing swords, daggers, maces, morning stars, and so on.

Ron Knight, "Medieval Weapons," 2000. www2.kumc.edu/instruction/academicsupport/itc/staff/rknight/Weapons.htm. Detailed description of armor, shields, and swords, and how they were used in battle.

Websites

English Heraldic Dictionary. jagor.srce.hr/~zheimer/heraldry/h.htm. Provides detailed descriptions, accompanied by colored diagrams, of heraldic designs.

The Knights Templar Preceptory. www.trantex.fi/staff/heikkih/knights/portcull.htm. Presents a wealth of information about the history, organization, weapons, battles, and final fate of the Knights Templars.

Books

Richard Barber, *The Knight and Chivalry*. Totowa, NJ: Rowman and Littlefield, 1974. Noteworthy study by an eminent historian on the nature of chivalry and the reality of its practice. Period illustrations and a thorough bibliography accompany the text.

Joachim Bumke, *The Concept of Knighthood in the Middle Ages*. Translated by W. T. H. Jackson and Erika Jackson. New York: AMS Press, 1982. A comprehensive study of knighthood in medieval Germany, supplemented by a good bibliography of both primary and secondary works.

Norman F. Cantor, *The Civilization of the Middle Ages*. New York: HarperCollins, 1993. A thorough, updated history of the Middle Ages by an important medieval scholar. The book provides facts and insights into the people and events of the whole period, useful reading lists, and a list of recommended films about the Middle Ages.

Andreas Capellanus, *The Art of Courtly Love*. Translated by John Jay Parry. New York: Norton, 1969. A famous twelfth-century discussion of the nature of courtly love and its traditions.

Geoffroi de Charny, *Book of Chivalry*. Translated by Richard W. Kaeuper and Elspeth Kennedy. Philadelphia: University of Pennsylvania Press, 1996. Written in the 1350s by a French knight, this account lays out the ground rules for knighthood and chivalry.

Heather Child, *Heraldic Design: A Handbook for Students*. London: George Bell, 1965. A profusely illustrated introduction to heraldry that presents various aspects of this complicated subject in clear, concise language.

S. D. Church, *The Household Knights of King John*. Cambridge: Cambridge University Press, 1999. Examines the life and duties of the knights who lived in the household of the English rulers John and Henry III.

Peter Coss, *The Knight in Medieval England: 1000–1400*. Phoenix Mill, England: Alan Sutton, 1993. Filled with photographs, drawings, and maps, this work traces the history of knighthood in medieval England.

George Gordon Coulton, trans. and ed., *Life in the Middle Ages*. New York: Macmillan, 1910. Contains hundreds of informative period documents covering every aspect of medieval life.

David Crouch, *William Marshall: Court, Career, and Chivalry in the Angevin Empire, 1147–1219*. London: Longman, 1990. A good, concise biography of an English knight who won fame as both a model of chivalry and as an astute politician.

Gutierre Díaz de Gómez, *The Unconquered Knight: A Chronicle of the Deeds of Don Pero Niño, Count of Buelna*. Translated and edited by Joan Evans. London: Routledge, 1928. A detailed account of the thirty-year career of fifteenth-century Spanish knight Don Pero Niño, who campaigned over much of western Europe.

Richard Phillipson Dunn-Pattison, *The Black Prince*. London: Methuen, 1910. This biography of Edward the Black Prince details the role of the son of King Edward III in the early English victories of the Hundred Years' War. Illustrations, maps, battle plans, and period documents are useful additions to the text.

David Edge and John Miles Paddock, *Arms and Armor of the Medieval Knight: An Illustrated History of Weaponry in the Middle Ages*. New York: Crescent Books, 1988. A thorough examination of the weapons and armor used throughout the Middle Ages. Full and half-page photographs, many in color, are effective companions to the text.

Jean Froissart, *Chronicles*. Translated by John Bourchier, Lord Berners, and edited by George Campbell Macaulay. London: Macmillan, 1895. An invaluable contemporary record of western Europe during the fourteenth century that gives much detailed, firsthand information about the people and events of the time, particularly the early battles of the Hundred Years' War.

François Louis Ganshof, *Feudalism*. 3rd ed. Translated by Philip Grierson. Toronto: University of Toronto Press, 1996. The first part of this well-known book is a good, sound history of the development of feudalism, and the second is a description of what the feudal system was and how it operated.

Frances Gies, *The Knight in History*. New York: Harper & Row, 1984. A thorough, but concise, history of medieval knighthood, from its beginning to its end. Numerous black-and-white plates and maps, as well as an extensive bibliography, supplement the text.

Joseph Gies and Frances Gies, *Life in a Medieval Castle*. New York: Harper & Row, 1979. A history of the castle, with particular emphasis on a knight's daily life and his household duties.

Charles Warren Hollister, Joe W. Leedom, and Marc A. Meyer, eds., *Medieval Europe: A Short Sourcebook*. New York: John Wiley, 1982. A useful, if limited, selection of original writings from the Middle Ages, most of which are modern translations.

Richard W. Kaeuper, *Chivalry and Violence in Medieval Europe*. Oxford: Oxford University Press, 1999. A modern look at chivalry and the degree to which it affected knightly conduct on and off the battlefield.

Maurice Keen, *Chivalry*. New Haven, CT: Yale University Press, 1984. A thorough study of the ideal and the reality of chivalric behavior during the Middle Ages. An extensive bibliography of primary and secondary sources, as well as photographs of medieval artifacts, augment the text.

Walter Clifford Meller, *A Knight's Life in the Days of Chivalry*. New York: AMS Press, 1924. A comprehensive, illustrated study of all aspects of medieval knighthood, filled with useful details of how knights trained, fought, and lived.

A. Vesey B. Norman and Don Pottinger, *A History of War and Weapons, 449–1660: English Warfare from the Anglo-Saxons to Oliver Cromwell*. New York: Thomas Y. Crowell, 1996. The chapters dealing with the Middle Ages discuss in detail the period's weapons. Drawings, many of them tinted, help show how these weapons were used.

Frederic Austin Ogg, ed., *A Source Book of Medieval History*. New York: Cooper Square Publishers, 1907. One of the best sources for original writings from the Middle Ages. Lengthy excerpts from medieval documents have thoughtful introductions explaining the importance of each selection.

Sidney Painter, *French Chivalry: Chivalric Ideas and Practices in Medieval France*.

Ithaca, NY: Cornell University Press, 1964. Examines the role chivalry played in the feudal system, as well as in the development of the courtly love tradition.

The Poem of the Cid. Translated by William Stanley Merwin. In *Medieval Epics*. New York: Modern Library, 1963. The twelfth-century epic that tells of the adventures of medieval Spain's most popular hero, the Cid, who battled both Christian and Muslim enemies.

The Rule of the Templars: The French Text of the Rule of the Order of the Knights Templar. Translated by Judith Mary Upton-Ward. Woodbridge, England: Boydell Press, 1992. Reproduces the regulations that governed the Knights Templars.

Aldo Scaglione, *Knights at Court: Courtliness, Chivalry, and Courtesy from Ottonian Germany to the Italian Renaissance*. Berkeley: University of California Press, 1991. Examines chivalry's effect upon social interactions among members of the knightly class, particularly those at royal courts in France, Germany, and Italy.

Desmond Seward, *The Monks of War: The Military Religious Orders*. Hamden, CT: Archon Books, 1972. Containing illustrations and maps, this survey covers the origins, structures, and purposes of the major knightly orders of the Middle Ages.

The Song of Roland. Translated by William Stanley Merwin. In *Medieval Epics*. New York: Modern Library, 1963. A prose translation of a very popular medieval epic poem about knighthood.

Peter Speed, ed., *Those Who Fought: An Anthology of Medieval Sources*. New York: Italica Press, 1996. A large selection of medieval writings on knighthood, chivalry, and battle.

The Statutes of the Realm: Printed by Command of His Majesty King George the Third, in Pursuance of an Address of the House of Commons of Great Britain, from Original Records and Authentic Manuscripts. 11 vols. London: Dawsons of Pall Mall, 1963. An invaluable collection of English public papers from the thirteenth through the eighteenth centuries.

Matthew Strickland, *War and Chivalry: The Conduct and Perception of War in England and Normandy, 1066–1217*. Cambridge: Cambridge University Press, 1996. This study of the Normans examines both their chivalric ideals and their actual practices in war.

Barbara W. Tuchman, *A Distant Mirror: The Calamitous 14th Century*. New York: Alfred A. Knopf, 1978. A superior, in-depth look at fourteenth-century Europe. Excellent research and fascinating speculation are embellished by lavish illustrations, maps, and an extensive bibliography.

Stephen Turnbull, *The Book of the Medieval Knight*. London: Arms and Armour Press, 1985. Embellished by many color and black-and-white plates, this study concentrates on knighthood in the fourteenth and fifteenth centuries.

Malcolm Vale, *War and Chivalry*. London: Duckworth, 1981. Describes how war was waged in the Middle Ages, and details the role of the knight in combat.

Donald A. White, ed., *Medieval History: A Source Book*. Homewood, IL: Dorsey Press, 1965. Period writings on feudalism, justice, military service, and the Crusades, among others.

Internet Sources

"Manual of Arms for the Axe," 1999. Translated by Sydney Anglo. www.thehaca.com. An anonymous fifteenth-century manual, detailing the use of a poleax, which combined elements of a spear and a battleax.

"Master Sigmund Ringeck's Commentaries on Johann Liechtenauer's Fechtbuch," 1999. Transated by Joerg Bellighausen and edited by J. Clements. www.thehaca.com/pdf/Ringeck.htm. One of the earliest surviving fighting manuals, in which the original author and his commentator, both master swordsmen, detail the ins and outs of medieval sword play. Accompanying the text are reproductions of the work's original woodcuts that illustrate the various positions and moves.

Index

Picture Credits

About the Author

James A. Corrick has been a professional writer and editor for twenty years and is the author of twenty-five books, as well as two hundred articles and short stories. Some of his other books for Lucent include *The Early Middle Ages*, *The Late Middle Ages*, *The Battle of Gettysburg*, *The Byzantine Empire*, *The Renaissance*, *The Industrial Revolution*, *The Civil War: Life Among the Soldiers and Cavalry*, and *The Louisiana Purchase*. Along with a Ph.D. in English, Corrick's academic background includes a graduate degree in the biological sciences. He has taught English, tutored minority students, edited magazines for the National Space Society, been a science writer for the Muscular Dystrophy Association, and edited and indexed books on history, economics, and literature for Columbia University Press, MIT Press, and others. He and his wife live in Tucson, Arizona.